BC TRIVIA

DON BLAKE

LONE PINE

Copyright © 1992 by Lone Pine Publishing
Printed in Canada
First printed in 1992 5 4 3 2 1
All rights reserved. No part of this work covered by the copyrights hereon may be reproduced or used in any form or by any means-graphic, electronic or mechanical-without the prior written permission of the publisher, except for reviewers who may quote brief passages.

The publisher:	The publisher:
Lone Pine Publishing	**Lone Pine Publishing**
206, 10426-81 Avenue	#202A, 1110 Seymoour St.
Edmonton, Alberta, Canada	Vancouver, B.C.
T6E 1X5	V6B 3N3

Canadian Cataloguing in Publication Data

Blake, Don, 1935-
   BC Trivia

First ed. has title: This is beautiful British Columbia.
Includes bibliographical references and index.
ISBN 1-55105-025-0
   1. British Columbia—Miscellanea. I. Title.
II. Title: This is beautiful British Columbia.
FC3811.B52 1992   971.1   C92-091795-X
F1087.B52 1992

Cover design & layout: B. Timothy Keith
Editorial: Philip Kennedy, Debby Shoctor
Printing: Friesen Printers, Altona, Manitoba, Canada

The publisher gratefully acknowledges the assistance of the Federal Department of Communications, Alberta Culture and Multiculturalism, the Canada Council, and the financial support provided by the Alberta Foundation for the Arts in the production of this book.

ACKNOWLEDGEMENTS

My special thanks to my willing and able secretary, assistant, partner, and wife, Donna. Thanks also to Pix-A-Color of Edmonton for photo processing and especially to Reg for his encouragement, advice, and answers to such questions as "What am I doing wrong?"; and to a great number of people all over the province who gave me information, directions and advice: Thank you all very much.

for

DJ

Rest in Peace
Little Guy

CONTENTS

Foreword 9

Symbols & Superlatives 11
Symbols • Superlatives

History 15
Ancient Times • The Coming of the White Man • Gold • Explorers & Statesmen • Sites

Government 17
The Government • Political History • Women in Politics

Services 20
Education • Medicine • Religion

Communications 25
Telegraphs • Telephones • Postal • Newspapers • Radio and Television

Transportation 27
Ships • Railways • Highways • Alaska Highway • Airways

Business & Industry 40
Forestry • Totem Poles • Mining • Geological Phenomena • Geologic Oddities • Fishing • Agriculture • Miscellaneous • Lotteries • Electrical Power • Tourism

Weather 52
Heat & Sun • Rain • Snow & Cold

Military 55

Sports 56
Skiing • Hockey • Football • Baseball • Games • Titles & Records • Odds & Ends

Law & Order 60
History • Facts

In & On The Water 63
Rivers • Lakes • Odds & Ends • Sport Fishing

Cities & Towns 67
Mottos and Slogans • Miscellaneous Names

Parks 73
National Parks • Provincial Parks

Arts & Entertainment 77
The Arts • Expo '86

Miscellaneous 81
Geography • Places • People • WildlifeRecords • Clocks

The Odd Spot 85

Odds & Ends 86
The Metric System • Time changes in British Columbia • Messages and Congratulations

Bibliography 91

Index 93

FOREWORD

SUPER, NATURAL BRITISH COLUMBIA

Anyone travelling around B.C. will soon discover why it is called both Super and Natural. Beauty, of course, is in the eye of the beholder, and in British Columbia, there is something for everyone.

From the plains of the northeast, through the Rocky Mountains, Interior Plateau, the Coast Mountains and the Islands, there is something for everyone. From desert and semi-arid lands to full thick rain forests, from the seashore to the mountain tops, from the big cities to vast uninhabited areas, there are many points in between to give pleasure to young and old, to amateur or professional. The diversity of this province's environment is reflected in the abundance and variety of its wildlife.

Whatever "your thing" is, you will certainly find it somewhere in this land of natural beauty. It has been said that the whole is no greater than the sum of its parts. B.C.'s many attractions add up to "Super" and "Natural."

The 1953 Gazeteer of Canada (B.C.) says, of B.C., "Its people have every right to enjoy a sense of pride of accomplishment for its foundations have been well and truly laid."

There are so many other points of interest in and around B.C. that I just couldn't begin to list them all here. Things like all the fabulous ski hills, golf courses, hiking trails, rafting and sailing, museums and zoos, gardens, the Royal Hudson, etc. So many exciting and challenging things to do and see in this western wonderland.

This book then is the how, what, why, where, when and the trivia of what made, or makes British Columbia. The statements, facts and figures are laid out in a general way according to subject. Facts and figures given are the latest available at the time of writing. The knowledge contained in this book is easily accessible to anyone looking for it. There is nothing new here except perhaps the way in which it has been compiled. If I have made any errors, or have offended anyone in any way, please accept my apologies.

And last I would like to add this. Most people judge a book, or whatever, by the extent to which it interests them. It is my sincerest wish that you find more points of interest in this book, than those which are not.

Don Blake

CHAPTER 1

SYMBOLS & SUPERLATIVES

SYMBOLS

The **Western Redcedar** (*Thuja Plicata Donn*) was adopted as the official tree of British Columbia on February 18, 1988. Historically, this tree has played an important role in the lives of west coast Indians and continues to be a valuable resource for the province.

Jade became the official mineral emblem in 1968. Consisting mostly of nephrite, B.C. jade is prized by carvers of fine jewellery and sculptures at home and abroad.

The **Pacific Dogwood** (*Cornus Nuttallii*) was adopted in 1956 as British Columbia's floral emblem. It grows 6 to 8 metres in height and flowers in April and May.

The **Stellar's Jay** (*Cyanacitta stelleri*) became B.C.'s official bird on December 17, 1987. Coloured a vibrant blue and black, it is found throughout the province. This lively bird was voted the most popular by the people of British Columbia.

The **Provincial Tartan** has five colours, each with its own significance: blue for the ocean; white for the Dogwood; green for the forests; red for the Maple Leaf; and gold for the crown and sun on the shield and flag. The tartan was adopted in 1974.

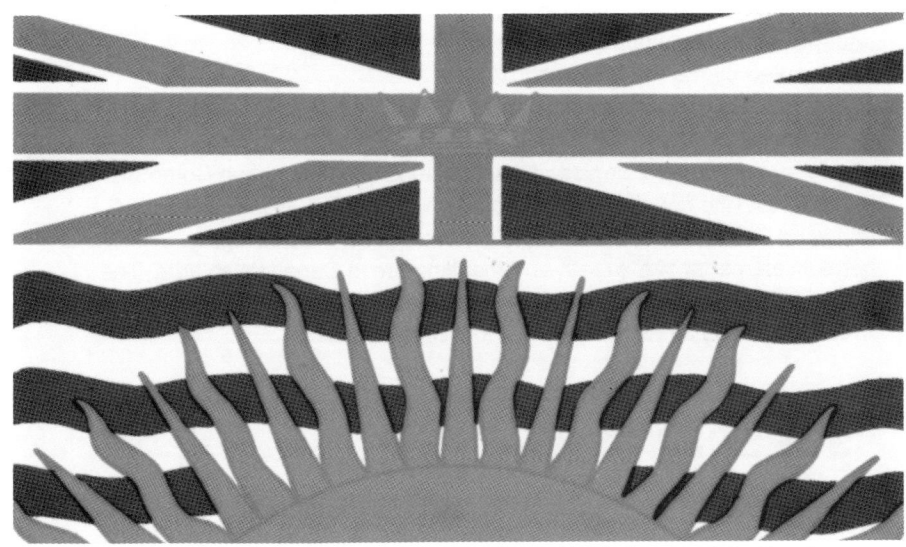

Adopted in 1960, the flag duplicates the design of the Shield of Arms of the Province. Its proportion is five by length and three by width.

THE LEGEND OF THE DOGWOOD

There is a legend that at the time of the crucifixion, the dogwood had been the size of the oak and other trees. So firm and strong, it was chosen as the timber for the cross. To be used for such a cruel purpose greatly distressed the tree, and Jesus, nailed upon it, sensed this, and in His gentle compassion for all sorrow and suffering, said to it "Because of your regret and pity for My suffering, never again shall the dogwood grow large enough to be used for a cross. Henceforth it shall be slender and twisted, and its blossoms in the form of a cross, at the outer edge of each petal shall be nail prints brown with rust and stained with red, and in the centre of the flower shall be a crown of thorns, and all who see shall remember."

The Shield of the Province of British Columbia was originally granted by King Edward VII in 1906; the remaining elements of the Coat of Arms were subsequently granted by Her Majesty Queen Elizabeth II on October 15, 1987. The Union Jack on the Shield symbolizes B.C.'s colonial origins. Its geographic location between the Pacific Ocean and the Rocky Mountains is represented by the wavy blue and silver bars and the setting sun. The supporters, the stag and the ram, represent the former colonies of Vancouver Island and British Columbia. The Royal Crest (the crowned lion standing on the crown), wears a collar of dogwood flowers, and sits atop the golden helmet of sovereignty. Traditional heraldic elements of a wreath and mantling are in Canada's colours. The provincial flower, the dogwood, appears a second time entwining the motto which translates as *"Splendour Without Diminishment."*

SUPERLATIVES

Demographics

B.C.'s population is **3,213,200** (est. 1991). *(Compare this to the City of Tokyo, with a population of 24 million.)*

There were 43,769 births in B.C. in 1989 and 22,997 deaths.

75% of B.C.'s population lives in the southwest corner of the province.

This third largest province, in area and population, has 38 cities, 14 towns, 46 villages, 49 districts, and 1 Indian government district.

Approximately **70% of B.C.'s population** lives on the lower mainland and southern Vancouver Island.

Geography

Canada's Economic Zone extends 322 km (200 mi.) from the surf line seawards. In effect, this means B.C. actually starts at a point 3,600 m (11,811 ft.) below the surface of the Pacific Ocean, 322 km offshore. There is a gradual rise to the -2500 m point and from here a very sharp upturn to about -200 m. From this point on to shore it is known as the "Continental Shelf." Within this area are some 6500 coastal islands, including Vancouver Island and the Queen Charlotte Islands, all of which are part of an ancient mountain range that lies mostly under the ocean.

Of the 33 highest mountains in Canada, nine are in B.C. Three of these are on the B.C.–Alaska border and one on the B.C.–Alberta border. The highest is **Mt. Fairweather** on the B.C.–Alaska border, which reaches a height of 4,663 m (15,300 ft.). It is the tenth highest in Canada. In B.C. the other eight are rated as 22nd, 23rd, 24th, 25th, 29th, 30th, 31st and 33rd highest in Canada.

The **highest mountain** wholly within British Columbia is Mt. Waddington, at 4,042 m (13,260 ft.), in the Coast Range Mountains. Straddling the B.C.–Alaska border is Mt. Fairweather 4,663 m (15,300 ft.), and across the B.C.–Alberta border is Mt. Robson., 3,954 m (12,972 ft.). The highest mountain in Canada is Mt. Logan, Yukon, 6,050m (19,850ft.).

British Columbia is on the northwest coast of North America. This **third largest province** of Canada lies between 114°03'12" W longitude in the southeast corner and 139°03'40" W longitude in the northwest corner, and between the latitudes of 48°17'34" N, in Juan de Fuca Strait, and 60° N.

British Columbia, with an **area of 952,263 km²** (approx. 367,697.5 sq. mi.), covers 9.5% of Canada's and 0.64% of the world's land surface.

B.C. is approximately 1450 km (900 mi.) in length from north to south and averages about 640 km (400 mi.) in width.

Comparisons

On the world scene British Columbia is four times larger than Great Britain, two and a half times as large as Japan, or equal to the combined size of France, Germany, Austria and Belgium. There are only thirty nations in the world bigger than British Columbia.

In the U.S.A. the only state **larger than B.C.** is Alaska which is 1.6 times B.C.'s size. B.C. is as big as Washington, Oregon and California combined. B.C. is about 1.35 times as big as Texas, and is larger than the combined areas of Connecticut, Delaware, Hawaii, Maryland, Massachusetts, New Hampshire, New Jersey, Rhode Island, Vermont, The

IN ROUGH FIGURES, BRITISH COLUMBIA CONSISTS OF:	
Provincial Forests	78.0%
Licensed Tree Farms	6.8%
Community Pastures	0.2%
Provincial Parks	5.6%
Crown Land (under Land Act Tenure)	0.4 %
Ecological Reserves (land only)	0.1%
Private Land	6.0%
Federal Land	1.0%
Water Area	1.9%

BORDER LENGTH

B.C. and Alberta	1,545 km (960 mi.)
B.C. and Alaska	893 km (555 mi.)
B.C. and Yukon	845 km (525 mi.)
B.C. and Washington State	423 km (263 mi.)
B.C. and N.W.T.	217 km (135 mi.)
B.C. and Montana	145 km (90 mi.)
B.C. and Idaho	72 km (45 mi.)

District of Columbia and Texas. There are nine states smaller than Vancouver Island. B.C. is over 7 times larger than the state of New York, which in population is over 6 times greater than B.C.. Its parklands total approximately 59,040 sq. km², which is larger than the five smallest states combined.

In Canada, B.C. is as big as the combined areas of Newfoundland, Nova Scotia, Prince Edward Island and Yukon. Vancouver Island is 5.5 times as large as P.E.I. and B.C.'s parkland is over 10 times the size of P.E.I.

A survey conducted throughout Canada in 1986 showed that while most Canadians would prefer to live where they were presently located, those who would move if they could, would first choose British Columbia. The west coast has also been called **the "rest coast,"** as many people go there to retire.

The Gazetteer of British Columbia (1985) shows there are about **42,350 geographical place names** in B.C.

Borders

B.C. is Canada's **gateway to the Pacific** and, as such, is Canada's gateway to the Pacific Rim, a fact of extreme importance to Canada's future economic development.

The boundary between Canada and the United States is 8,891 km (5,526 mi.) long and is maintained by a survey network, established by these two countries, of one thousand survey control stations along its length. Boundary markers are spaced at distances of 1.6 to 2.4 km (1 to 1 1/2 mi.)

The Canada-United States boundary is "out" about 244 m (800 ft.) at the Douglas-Blaine crossing. This error is in the favour of the United States. Near Sweetgrass, Montana, it is out about 366 m (1200 ft.) but this time in Canada's favour. The overall picture of the 49th parallel boundary location is that it is about 24 to 25 metres (80 ft.) in Canada's favour. This boundary was first surveyed and laid out in the 1850's and these errors were the result of "gravity anomalies." These **boundary discrepancies** are mentioned here only as a point of interest. The legal boundary is the

B.C.'S...

Most easterly point	Akamina Pass Area	114°03'12" W
Most westerly point	Boundary Peak	139°03'40" W
Most southerly point	Rosedale Rock, Vancouver Isl.	48°17'34" N
Most northerly point	Beaver River Area	60°00'09" N
Longest Valley	Rocky Mt. Trench	1450 km (900 mi.)
Highest City	Kimberley	1115 m (3660 ft.)
Largest Coastal Island	Vancouver Island	32,137 km² (12,408 sq. mi.)
Number of Coastal Islands		Approx. 6,500 (excluding islets)
Length of Mainland Coast		Approx. 12,150 km (7,550 mi.)
Length of Coast *(including islands)*		Approx. 27,200 km (16,900 mi.)
Longest Inlet *(fjord, channel)*	Gardner Canal	Approx. 114 km (71 mi.)
Deepest Recorded Sounding *(of coastal area)*	Finlayson Channel	764 m (2508')

ROYAL VISITS

1901	Duke and Duchess of Cornwall and York *(the future King George V and Queen Mary)*
1919	The Prince of Wales *(the future King Edward VII)*
1939	King George VI and Princess Elizabeth
1951	Princess Elizabeth and Prince Philip
1959	Queen Elizabeth II and Prince Philip
1971	Queen Elizabeth II and Prince Philip
1983	Queen Elizabeth II and Prince Philip
1986	Prince Charles and Princess Diana
1987	Queen Elizabeth and Prince Philip

one in place, on the ground, where we know and see it today. Other points are simply on paper and of interest only to those involved with the earth sciences.

In the fall of 1914 a large gathering at the border celebrated 100 years of peace between Canada and the United States. As a result of this gathering, the **International Peace Arch** was built at the border crossing of Blaine, Washington and Douglas, B.C. in 1920-21. It is the only arch of its kind in the world and was built by Americans and Canadians using cement and steel which had been donated. It was dedicated September 6, 1921 by Samuel Hill from the United States and Premier John Oliver of B.C.

On Saturday July 2, 1927, five thousand residents of Canada and the United States gathered at the Peace Arch at Douglas/Blaine, to inaugurate the first **International Flag Day**, a gesture pledging and cementing perpetual friendship and goodwill between the two countries. This event is carried out annually on the second Sunday of June. In Washington State this has been declared "Peace Arch Sunday."

The Douglas/B.C.-Blaine/Washington border crossing south of Vancouver is one of the busiest in Canada. During 1990 approximately 10.4 million people went through this Canada Customs checkpoint.

CHAPTER 2

HISTORY

ANCIENT TIMES

During the last few million years, there have been several **ice ages**. The last one was some 18,000 years ago and its retreat was not complete in some places, until as recently as 5,000 or 6,000 years ago. At times, and in certain areas, the ice may have been more than a kilometre thick.

Barbara Ronald of Saanich, B.C., found the 17,000 year old **fossilized tooth** of an extinct woolly mammoth, while she was walking down the Island View Beach near her home in 1990. It is the best preserved specimen yet to be found. She had noticed it on a previous walk but, by the grooves on it, thought is was a side of ribs from a dead animal, and side stepped it. Archaeologists say that this is the oldest large-mammal fossil ever to be discovered on Vancouver Island.

A bear skull about 9,400 years old was found in a huge cave complex on Vancouver Island.

According to archaeologists, some **ancient Indian sites** in B.C. are over 9,000 years old.

There is evidence to suggest the **Chinese** may have visited the coast of British Columbia as early as 500 AD.

THE COMING OF THE WHITE MAN

Historians disagree on how far north **Francis Drake** sailed in 1579, but there is a possibility he neared what is now the southern B.C. coast. He may have been the first white man to see this province. A 2,200 m (7,219 ft.) high peak on Vancouver Island is named for his ship, the Golden Hinde. Also on board were George Vancouver and William Bligh.

The **first white man** to actually live in B.C. was John Mackay. He spent a year at Nootka (1787-88) and then left with Captain Charles William Barkley, who was buying furs from the Natives for resale in China. When she was 17 years old, Captain Barkley's wife, Frances, became the first white woman to set foot on Vancouver Island.

The **first white man** to set foot on British Columbian soil was Captain James Cook.

"**Alexander MacKenzie**, from Canada, by land, July 22, 1793". These words were painted by Mackenzie on a large rock on Dean Channel near Bella Coola, B.C., thus completing the first overland crossing of the North American continent by a white man. Mackenzie was acting on behalf of the North West Company, which was searching for river

A "Hand of History" sign at Kitwanga, B.C.. An interesting and historic area.

STORIES IN CEDAR

"The glories of war and the legends of the people are told in the crests of the British Columbia natives. One above the other, each crest adds a chapter to the story on the totem. Raven, Frog, Wolf, Fireweed, and Eagle carved in cedar logs tell the history of the family groups they represent. Crest-winning and slave-taking were important rituals in warfare. Because individual crests belong to a particular family, winning these crests brought prestige to those who won them."
Sign at Kitwanga, B.C.

routes that would give its traders access to Pacific furs. He journeyed through B.C. along the Peace, Parsnip and Fraser Rivers, and then travelled 15 days westward to the Bella Coola River.

David Stuart (or Stewart) and Alexander Ross of the Pacific Fur Company were the first white men to have travelled through the **Okanagan Valley**. During 1811 they were searching for a suitable site to establish a trading post; on May 16, 1812 they settled on the south side of the junction of the North and South Thompson Rivers. The city of Kamloops was later incorporated here in 1893.

GOLD

• The **first gold rush** to B.C. was a minor event occurring in 1851 when gold quartz was discovered at Mitchell's Harbour (or Gold Harbour) on the west coast of the Queen Charlotte Islands.
• Although gold and rumours of gold began to attract prospectors to mainland B.C. as early as 1855, the main rush began in 1858 on the Fraser and ultimately reached the Cariboo.
• Gold was discovered, in 1861, in the area north of British Columbia known as Stikine Territory.

EXPLORERS & STATESMEN

The **first ship to be built** on the west coast of North America, other than native craft, was the North West America. It was built under the direction of Lieutenant John Meares and launched Sept. 20, 1788 at Nootka Sound. Most of the work was done by Chinese craftsmen, specially brought for that purpose. The famous Native chief, Maguinna, was an interested spectator.

Vancouver Island was originally "**Quadra and Vancouver's Island**" named by Capt. George Vancouver about 1793. The area which is now northern Washington and southern B.C. he named "New Georgia." The coastal areas further north he called "New Hanover." H.B.C. fur traders didn't care for these names and continued to call the areas "Oregon" or "Columbia."

In 1808, when **Simon Fraser** was coming down the river which now bears his name, he called this region "New Caledonia."

David Thompson was one of Canada's **greatest geographers** and cartographers. Starting at Churchill, Manitoba at the age of 14, he surveyed and mapped more of Canada than anyone else. In 1811 he completed his survey of the Columbia River by travelling 1,851 km (1,150 mi.) to the Pacific Ocean. The Thompson River was named after him by Simon Fraser.

SITES

The **first trading post** established on the Columbia River was Kootenae House, near the present town of Invermere, in 1807.

The **stone cairn** at Fort Alexandria commemorates the last North West Company fur trading post to be established west of the Rockies. It was built in 1821.

Fort Langley was established by James McMillan in 1827 for the H.B.C. It was relocated to its present site in 1839.

A cairn marking the site of Fort Alexandria about 67 km. north of Williams Lake

Victoria began as **Fort Victoria**, built by the Hudson's Bay Company in 1843, but came into prominence only after the boundary between the U.S. and Britain was settled. The H.B.C. at this time moved its principal location on the west coast from Fort Vancouver on the Columbia River to Fort Victoria.

On June 15, 1846, the 49th parallel was decided upon as **the boundary** between the U.S. and the British Colonies. This line extends west from the Rocky Mountains to the Pacific Ocean then south and again west through Juan de Fuca Strait, leaving all of Vancouver Island in British hands. Many felt at the time the boundary line should have followed the Columbia River to the Pacific.

GOVERNMENT

In 1852 the Queen Charlotte Islands became a dependency of the Crown Colony of Vancouver Island.

In 1858 Queen Victoria decided the name "New Caledonia" was inappropriate and, at her suggestion, the **new colony of "British Columbia"** was proclaimed. The official ceremonies were conducted Nov. 19, 1858 at Fort Langley by James Douglas. He then appointed Mr. Matthew Baillie Begbie as Chief Justice of British Columbia and swore in James Douglas as Governor of British Columbia, thus making him the "Father" of our land.

◆

New Westminster became the **capital of B.C.** in early 1859.

◆

The federal post office in downtown New Westminster marks the location of the **first government buildings** in the city. On this site, in 1859, stood the government mint, assay office and land registry.

FUR, GOLD, AND CATTLE

A sign at Lookout Point in Kamloops states:
Founded in 1812, Fort Kamloops stood at a natural crossroads. For 50 years it remained the focus of an inland fur empire until the roaring mining boom of the 1860s. Ranchers, with cattle and horses, replaced the miners. They settled, and stayed, to see two railways bring prosperity anew to this land of sagebrush, sun, and great rivers.
Courtesy of B.C. Dept. of Recreation & Conservation

This sign, found north of Bonners Ferry in Idaho shows the impact that David Thompson had in mapping and exploring not only British Columbia but also south into the United States.

In 1862 the **Territory of Stikine** was established by Imperial Order in Council.

◆

In 1863 Stikine Territory and the Queen Charlotte Islands **united** with British Columbia.

◆

The Crown Colonies of British Columbia and Vancouver Island **were united** Nov. 19, 1866 with New Westminster as capital and F. Seymour as Governor.

◆

In 1866 the Rocky Mountains were designated as British Columbia's **eastern boundary**. The boundary line followed the "Continental Divide", from the U.S. border (the 49th parallel) north-west to 120° longitude (at approx. 54° latitude) from where it stretched north to 60° latitude.

During May of 1868 the **capital of British Columbia** was moved from New Westminster to Victoria.

◆

British Columbia became the **sixth province** of the Dominion of Canada on July 20, 1871. Upon acceptance into Canada a new constitution was proclaimed, giving British Columbia's Legislative Assembly 25 members: 12 from Vancouver Island and 13 from the mainland. At the time of its union with Canada, B.C.'s white population was less than 20,000.

◆

In 1872 three German judges, asked by Britain and the U.S. to settle the **boundary dispute** in Georgia Strait, ruled in favour of the U.S., giving them the San Juan Islands. B.C.'s southern boundary, as we now know it, was thus established.

◆

The boundary between B.C. and Alaska was decided in 1903.

CHAPTER 3

POLITICAL

THE GOVERNMENT

British Columbia has 32 seats in the **House of Commons** and 6 seats in the Senate.

The **Provincial Legislature** in Victoria has 75 seats.

The **Lieutenant Governor** is the legal head of the Provincial Executive.

POLITICAL HISTORY

Colonial

The **first Governor** of Vancouver Island was Richard Blanshard, from July 16, 1849 to August 30, 1851.

The **first Governor** of British Columbia was James Douglas, from September 2, 1858 to April 21, 1864.

The **first Governor** of the United Colonies of British Columbia and Vancouver Island was Frederick Seymour, from October 24, 1866 to June 10, 1869.

The **longest non-stop speech** in Canada was delivered by Leanard McLure, a member of the colonial legislature in

Sir James Douglas, "The Father of British Columbia."

British Columbia in 1866. McLure spoke for 16 hours without a break, fighting a property tax bill. A colleague followed with a seven hour speech. The government withdrew the bill.

Provincial

The **first Premier** of British Columbia was John Foster McCreight, from November 13, 1871 to December 20, 1872.

Amor de Cosmos means "Love of the Universe." Formerly known as Bill Smith of Nova Scotia, he changed his name before entering B.C. politics and becoming Premier 1872-74. He was one of the prime movers in the push to bring B.C. into the Canadian Confederation.

In 1872, due to continuing troubles with the Natives, particularly of the northern tribes, Dr. I. W. Powell was appointed the **first Superintendent of Indian Affairs**.

The Hon. Richard McBride, of New Westminster, became Premier of British Columbia on June 1, 1903. At the age of 32, he was the **youngest first minister** ever chosen in Canada.

In 1924 an organization called the **British Columbia Youth Parliament** was formed. It consists of students from all over the province who act out the various functions of our provincial parliament. The first Premier of this Parliament was 20-year-old Walter S. Owen. He went on to become the Lt. Governor of B.C. from Feb. 13, 1973 to May 19, 1978. The Youth Parliament is still active today.

The **first Sikh-Canadian** elected to a provincial legislature in Canada was Moe Sihota of Esquimalt-Port Renfrew on Vancouver Island during the provincial election of October, 1986.

During the 1991 Provincial Election in B.C., the New Democratic Party went from 25 seats to 51 seats to form a **majority government**. The Liberals went from 0 to 17 seats to form the official opposition and the Social Credit Party went down from 41 to seven seats.

Federal

In 1871 under the terms of the union of B.C. with Canada, **three senators** were appointed to represent British Columbia at Ottawa. They were: Dr. R. W. Carroll, C. F. Cornwall and W. J. MacDonald.

The **first Lt. Governor** of British Columbia was Joseph W. Trutch, July 5, 1871 - June 26, 1876.

The **first MPs** to represent B.C. in Ottawa, in the Parliament of 1872, were J. S. Thompson representing Cariboo, Hugh Nelson representing New Westminster, Robert Wallace representing Vancouver Island, Chas. F. Houghton representing Yale, Henry Nathan and Amor De Cosmos representing Victoria.

Canadians of Japanese ancestry were given the right to vote in March 1949.

Canada's **first Chinese MP** was elected in 1957. He was PC candidate Douglas Jung of Vancouver Centre.

In June of 1968 Len Marchand (Kamloops-Cariboo) became **the first Native** to be elected to the House of Commons, Ottawa.

Civic

In 1958 Peter Wing became the **first Chinese mayor** of any B.C. municipality when he was elected in Kamloops.

On Nov. 19, 1977 a **record voter turnout** for a B.C. community was established at Gabriola Island. Ninety-nine percent of the electorate (754 out of 761 voters) cast their ballots.

The local residents of Hosmer call their area the "Principality of Hosmer." The Mayor is elected every year at the Elk River Inn. Electors buy their votes by contributing to the local volunteer fire department at the rate of a penny per vote. A person may vote as many times as he wishes. For the winner, one of the conditions of the contract is that the Mayor is not allowed to do anything, in any official capacity, for his term of office. In 1984 Granville Burk was elected and impeached the same night for "peeing" on the bar room floor. Granville Burk was a dog.

WOMEN IN POLITICS

B.C's Women were given **the right to vote** in federal elections in 1917.

Mary Ellen Smith's election to the B.C. legislature in 1918 made her the **first female member** of that body. Three years later, her appointment as Minister Without Portfolio made her the **first female cabinet minister** in Canada. In 1928 she became the first woman to sit in the Speaker's chair in a British Parilament.

Mrs. Tilly Rolston was named Education Minister in the new Social Credit government, sworn in Aug. 1, 1952. This made her Canada's **first female Cabinet Minister With Portfolio**.

Rita Johnson became the 29th Premier of B.C., and the **first female Premier of a Canadian province**, on April 2, 1991. She was sworn in just after Bill Vander Zalm resigned because of conflict-of-interest charges over the sale of Fantasy Gardens in Richmond B.C

In 1888, the first parliament buildings in British Columbia were known as the "birdcages."

CHAPTER 4

SERVICES

EDUCATION

History

The Hudson's Bay Company, under the direction of Governor James Douglas of the Colony of Vancouver Island, established several schools in the Fort Victoria area as early as 1852. **Craigflower School**, at Victoria, opened in 1853. The present Craigflower School building was not completed until 1855 and is now considered to be the oldest school still standing in Western Canada. It closed in 1911, but reopened as a museum in 1931. It is located on the Craigflower Heritage Site, five kilometers from Victoria. The first teacher at Craigflower was Charles Clark.

St. Mary's Mission was founded by the Oblates of Mary Immaculate (OMI) in 1861 and was the **first, and largest, native residential school** of its kind in the Pacific Northwest. Located on the east side of Mission, B.C., the school was rebuilt by the federal government in 1959.

Public administration of education began in 1872 in British Columbia. **The first Superintendent of Schools** for the province was John Jessop.

The **first high school** in British Columbia opened in Victoria in 1876.

The **University of Victoria** started as Victoria College in 1903. The Universities Act of 1963 granted autonomy to the University of Victoria on July 1, 1963.

The **oldest schoolhouse** on B.C.'s mainland is on Pleasant Valley Road in Armstrong. It was built in 1884 and still contains some of its original artifacts.

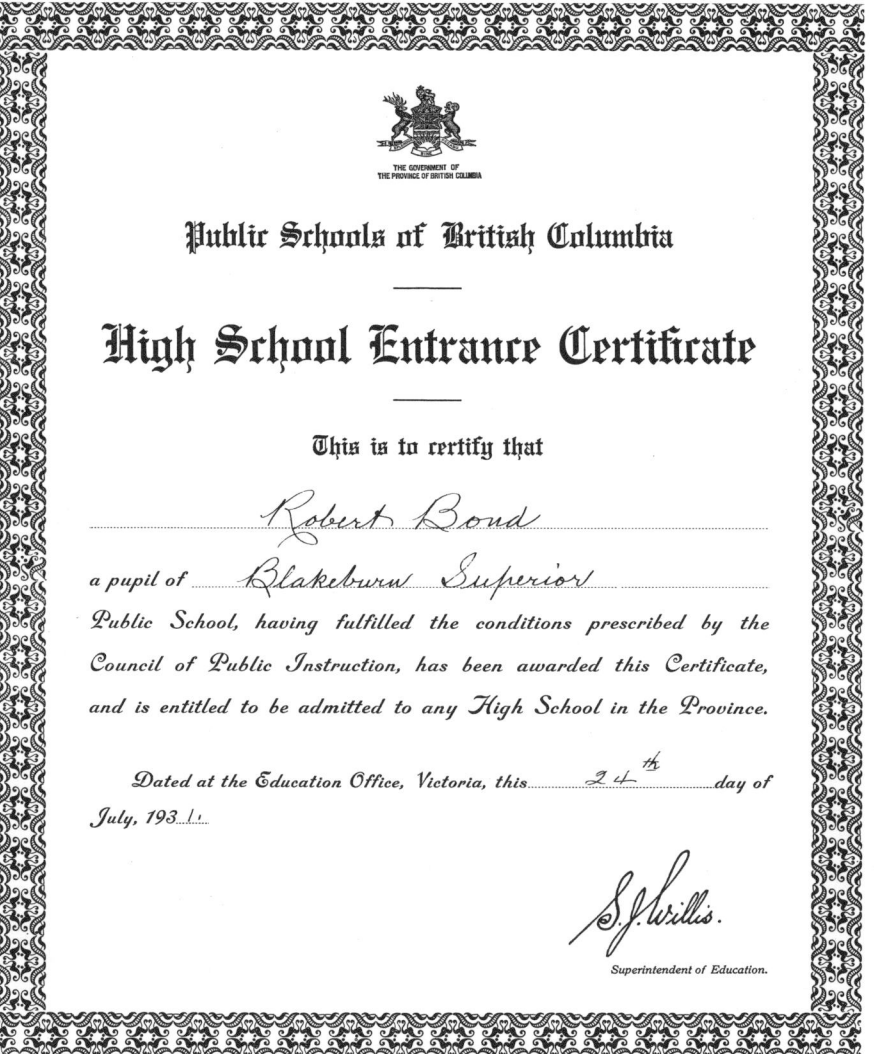

This 1931 certificate was granted to Bob Bond to enable him to attend any high school in B.C. The town of Blakeburn, where Mr. Bond fulfilled the necessary requirements, became a "ghost town" in 1940.

Higher education in British Columbia had its start in 1899.

In 1906 the **first Japanese school** in Canada opened in Vancouver's "Little Tokyo" area.

The first convocation of the **University of British Columbia** was held in 1912.

Simon Fraser University opened its doors Sept. 9, 1965.

Selkirk College, opened in December 1966 at Castlegar, was the first regional college in B.C.

B.C. HAS:

1,580	Public Schools
267	Independent Schools
15	Community Colleges
5	Technical Institutes
3	Public Universities
1	Private University

ENROLLMENT
in B.C.'s three Public Universities (*Fall 1989*):

University of B.C.	28,461
Simon Fraser University	15,923
University of Victoria	13,258
Total Enrollment	57,642

Education Facts

There are **75 school districts** in British Columbia administered by locally-elected boards of trustees.

The **University of Northern British Columbia** (UNBC) is Canada's newest university. Its main campus is in Prince George and it offers graduate programs and research with an emphasis on subjects relevant to northern British Columbia.

Public schools in British Columbia have approximately 513,533 pupils.

Trinity Western University, a private university, has a student population of 1,300 graduates and undergraduates.

In 1989, astronomers at the University of Victoria **redefined the age of the universe** and discovered the first evidence of planets around other stars.

The only provincial governments in Canada to operate their own **educational TV networks** are British Columbia, Alberta, Ontario and Quebec.

British Columbia has established **The Open Learning Agency**, which coordinates open learning programs and services in the province for the provision of distance education. "The Agency is comprised of three components: the Open University, the Open College and the Knowledge Network."

There are over **80,000 employees** in B.C.'s various education systems.

British Columbia's **educational costs** for the fiscal year 1990-91 were estimated to be $4,137,000,000.00.

MEDICINE

History

The **first hospital** in British Columbia was established in 1858 in the home of the Rev. E. Cridge at Fort Victoria.

Dr. J.S. Helmcken was British Columbia's **first resident physician**. His home, in Victoria, is the oldest residence in the province serving its original function on its original site.

From the *British Columbian*, June 22, 1862: "**First British Columbia twins:** Twin boys were born at the Royal Engineers camp on the 3d inst. This we understand is the first case of twins in the Colony and makes the number of children at the R.E. Camp 99. Rumor says the even hundred will not long be wanting."

The Royal Columbian Hospital, founded in 1862, is **the oldest hospital** on B.C.'s mainland. Replacing a military infirmary, the original 30-bed hospital was built in New Westminster. In 1889 the hospital moved to its present location in Sapperton. The Royal Columbian Hospital today is one of the largest referral hospitals in B.C.

On August 24, 1863, Judge Begbie laid the first foundation log for the Royal Caribou Hospital, **the first hospital serving the goldfield towns** along Williams Creek. As the communities matured, the second Royal Caribou Hospital was built around 1891. It served the area for over 40 years until destroyed by fire in March, 1936.

Vancouver's first hospital opened in 1886 with a nine-bed structure erected by the C.P.R. for its workmen.

Facts

The **worst poliomyelitis epidemic** in B.C.'s history was in 1952 with 580 cases reported including 36 deaths.

The **largest General Hospital** in B.C. is the Vancouver General Hospital (VGH), with 913 acute care beds.

In B.C. more deaths result from **avalanches** than from any other natural hazard. Avalanches have killed over 100 people.

B.C. HAS:

		Beds
97	Acute Care Hospitals	11,365
2	Federal Hospitals	
15	Diagnostic and Treatment Centres	
5	Free Standing Rehabilitation Hospitals	428
5	Extended Care Hospitals	7,801
6	Red Cross Outposts	

There are 7,200 **Doctors** in B.C.

There are 1,989 **Dentists** in B.C.

There are 32,789 **registered nurses (R.N.s)** in B.C.

There are 486 licensed **graduate nurses** in B.C.

Health care in B.C. for the 1990-91 fiscal year was estimated at $4,891,000,000.00.

The Medical Services Plan of British Columbia, offering comprehensive coverage of medical care as well as supplementary services, **covers over 98% of all the people** in the province.

The **largest AIDS study program** in Canada is being conducted at U.B.C.

A bar in Nanaimo, B.C. **charges smokers 25 cents** to rent an ashtray. The proceeds go to the Canadian Cancer Society.

RELIGION

History

The **first religious service in B.C.** was a mass celebrated at Nootka on June 24, 1789 by Father Lopez Di Nava and Father Mario Diaz. They were chaplains on Capt. Jose Martinez' ship, the Santiago. It had previously been thought that the first religious service had been conducted on Sunday Oct. 14, 1838 at

ACROSS CANADA FUNDRAISERS

MARATHON OF HOPE

Terry Fox and his "Marathon of Hope" probably raised more funds and public awareness than any other individual effort in the fight against cancer. By November, 1984 contributions to the four-year-old Terry Fox fund for cancer research totalled $37 million. In addition to becoming the youngest member of the Order of Canada he also received the following awards:

Companion of the Order of Canada	1980
British Columbia Order of the Dogwood	1980
Canadian of the Year	1980 & 1981
Lou Marsh Award:	
Canada's Outstanding Athlete	1980
Canadian Sports Hall of Fame	1981
American Cancer Society Sword of Hope	
Guinness Book of World Records	

JOURNEY FOR LIVES

Inspired by the Terry Fox "Marathon of Hope," Steve Fonyo began his "Journey For Lives" at St. John's Newfoundland, on March 31, 1984. He paused briefly on December 1, 1984, at the Terry Fox monument in Thunder Bay, Ontario to lay a wreath of B.C. holly for his predecessor who had been forced to abandon his run at this point.

Public awareness took a considerable leap when Steve crossed the Ontario-Manitoba border and he reached his first million dollar mark in Saskatchewan. On April 23, 1985, he reached his home province of British Columbia and on May 27, 1985, he ran into B.C. Place Stadium, Vancouver, to the cheers of thousands of his fans. Two days later, May 29, he reached mile "0" at Beacon Hill Park, Victoria. His efforts have resulted in about $13 million dollars for cancer research.

MAN IN MOTION

On May 22, 1987 over 10,000 people were on hand at Oakridge Shopping Centre, in Vancouver, to welcome home Rick Hansen after his 26 month, 40,000 km, round the world, "Man in Motion" tour for spinal cord research. To date (Spring 1991), Rick Hansen's efforts have raised over $23 million for this cause.

Boat Encampment (on the Columbia River's "Big Bend" near the modern Mica Dam) by Fathers F.N. Blanchet and Modeste Demers as they passed through on their way to Oregon.

The oldest church on the B.C. mainland and still on its original foundations, is St. John the Divine Anglican Church in Yale.

The Chinese Freemasons' first lodge in Canada was established at Barkerville in 1863 as the Chi Kung Tong. This first temple served a number of purposes: a court to settle community disputes; an employment bureau; funeral home; church; medical clinic; community centre, etc. It burnt down in the Barkerville fire of Sept. 16, 1868 but was immediately rebuilt. The organization is still active.

The marine ministry of the United Church of Canada began in 1884 with the MV Gladtidings. Since that time they have used the services of some 37 vessels to bring religious guidance to isolated communities along the British Columbia coast. The most famous of these boats were probably the Thomas Crosby class.

St. Peter's Church was built in 1887 in the railway community of Donald and consecrated in 1889. Ten years later the C.P.R. decided to change their railway divisional point from Donald to Revelstoke. Most of the residents moved, along with their homes and commercial buildings, but the church "vanished." Acting without permission from church authorities, Rufus Kimpton, a local Donald merchant, had it dismantled and transported, piece by piece, by railway to Golden and by barge from there,

This beautiful church is at Skookumchuck (N. of Port Douglas.) The bottom section of the three steeples are painted red and all the rest of the building is white.

185 km (115 mi.) to the south, up the Columbia River and across Lake Windemere. The entire church was reassembled on a hillside overlooking the lake, where it still stands today. Outside is a cairn, commemorating the Rev. Henry "Father Pat" Irwin, vicar of the church when it was stolen. When the church was being transferred from the railway to the barges, at Golden, the church's 600 lb. bell was stolen. It later turned up in St. Paul's Church in Golden.

Facts

The **only Benedictine Monastery in B.C.** was established in 1954 on a hill above Mission, B.C., overlooking the Fraser Valley. There are only two such monasteries in Canada.

On September 18, 1984, the visit of Pope John Paul II brought together the largest crowd ever assembled for a single purpose in B.C. An estimated 200,000 people came together on the 485 ha (1200 acre) site at Abbotsford airport. 63,000 parking spaces, 2500 toilets and 33 concession stands were also set up. Later in the day the Pope's visit to B.C. Place Stadium was witnessed by about 65,000.

The Church of St. Saviour, the Barkerville Anglican Church was erected in 1869.

The **first Ismaili Mosque** to be built in North America was officially opened in Burnaby, B.C. August 23, 1985 by His Highness The Aga Khan and Canada's Prime Minister.

CHAPTER 5

COMMUNICATIONS

TELEGRAPHS

The **first magnetic dispatch** over British soil on the Pacific, was on April 3, 1865 between New Westminster and Government House a mile away. It was claimed that numerous messages were transmitted but none were suitable for publication.

On September 24, 1901, the **first messages** were transmitted over the new two thousand mile long telegraph line between Vancouver and Dawson City.

The city of New Westminster had a **telegraph office** in continuous operation for 113 years: 1865 to 1978. It was closed on April 10, 1978 due to a steadily decreasing number of telegrams in the past few years mainly because of the telephone and telex.

TELEPHONES

There are two stories of the **first telephone in B.C.** One story is that the first two telephones were hand made in 1877 to connect the Wellington Coal Mine with Departure Bay. The second story says the first telephone in B.C. was shown in a demonstration in the office of the Colonist newspaper in Victoria in March 1878.

The first telephone company in B.C., the Victoria and Esquimalt Telephone Co., was incorporated in 1880. It had 46 subscribers.

At the turn of the century there were about **45 telephone companies** in B.C. The Vernon and Nelson Telephone Company was probably the biggest and it was from this one that today's B.C. Tel originated. They were incorporated on April 20, 1891.

On April 1, 1903, B.C.'s **first private telephone exchange** was installed by the New Westminster and Burrard Inlet Telephone Co. on the premises of Hastings Shingle Manufacturing Co.

The **first overseas phone call**, from Vancouver to London, was made on March 9, 1928 via Halifax, Nova Scotia.

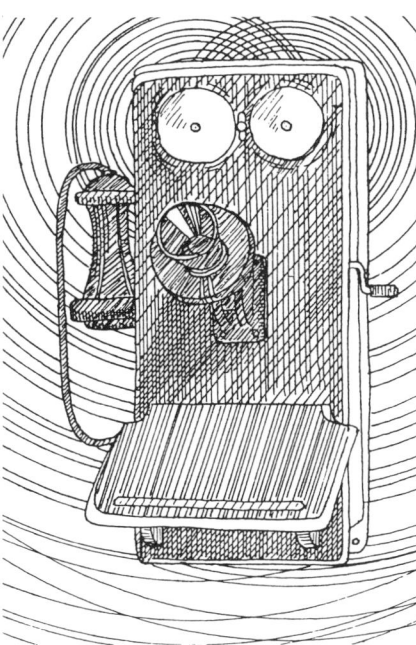

The **first dial telephones in B.C.** went into operation in Vancouver on Dec. 2, 1939.

The **first push button telephones** came into use in B.C. during 1971.

The world's **longest submarine telecommunications cable** was inaugurated simultaneously in Burnaby, Fiji, Australia, New Zealand and England on Nov. 7, 1984. It is 15,000 km long and can carry 1,380 simultaneous telephone conversations.

B.C. Telephone Co. Ltd., in 1990, was one of the **largest telecommunications companies** in Canada. During 1990 there were 1.92 million customer access lines in service with the B.C. Tel system, through which 357 million toll calls were completed. Regular full time employees numbered 14,997.

In B.C. there are **53 phone lines per 100 people** - this is higher than in any other province. The national rate is 48.9 lines per 100.

The world's **oldest and largest telephone booth** is located outside of the Sal-Crest Motel at Salmo, B.C. It was carved out of the trunk of a giant cedar tree.

POSTAL

The **first mail delivery** in B.C. arrived on the HMS Daedalus at Nootka's Friendly Cove on Vancouver Island, July 1792. It brought two letters, one for Capt. George Vancouver and the other for Commodore Juan Francisco de la Bodega y Quadra. The letters contained the message for Vancouver and orders to Bodega y Quadra to turn over Spanish possessions in the Pacific Northwest to Britain.

NEWSPAPERS

In 1843 **the first printing press** to be brought to Vancouver's Island arrived with Bishop Demers of the Roman Catholic Church at the newly founded Fort Victoria. This press printed the first newspaper in B.C., the French-language *Le Courier de la Nouvelle Caledonie*; the first book in B.C., The Fraser River Mines Vindicated by Alfred Waddington; the first issues of the Victoria Colonist and the first issues of the Cariboo Sentinel at Barkerville on June 6, 1865. This press is now one of the treasured possessions of the Sisters of St. Anne in Victoria. It is on permanent display in the Provincial Museum at Victoria.

The Columbian printed its final edition Nov. 15, 1983. By some accounts its first edition was Feb. 13, 1861. It seems, however, that it was first printed as the New Westminster Times in 1859. Shortly thereafter it was renamed the British Columbian and later the Columbian. It was **B.C.'s oldest daily**.

Victoria's first newspaper, the *Victoria Gazette*, began in June 1858.

Vancouver's first newspaper was the *Vancouver Weekly Herald* starting Jan. 15, 1886.

RADIO AND TELEVISION

The highlight of the Diamond Jubilee of Confederation celebrations carried out across Canada on July 1, 1927, was the **first coast to coast radio network broadcast.**

The Canadian Association of Broadcasters warned in 1950, that the **introduction of television** would "unquestionably cripple" and possibly destroy AM radio broadcasting.

The Canadian Broadcasting Corporation opened Vancouver's **first French language station**, CBUF-FM on December 2, 1967.

There are **91 private originating radio stations** in British Columbia.

Although television was actually invented back in the 1920's, it was not until 1948 that Vancouver received its **first television broadcasts** (and these originated in Seattle, Washington).

There are now **8 television stations** in B.C.

Over 82% of British Columbia homes have **cable television**.

There are now **67 AM radio stations** in B.C. and **18 FM radio stations**.

CHAPTER 6

TRANSPORTATION

SHIPS

History

The Beaver was the **first steamship on the Pacific Ocean.** She was built in England and sailed around Cape Horn in 1835 to Fort Vancouver on the Columbia River. Here she was fitted as a steamer for the Hudson's Bay Company and set off on her maiden steam voyage on June 18, 1836. She had a crew of 31, including 4 stokers and 13 woodcutters, and burned, on the average, 7 to 8 cords of wood per day. *The Beaver* crashed and foundered on the rocks of Stanley Park's Prospect Point in 1888.

From 1858 up to the present time, B.C. waters have had **more paddlewheelers** (over 300) than any other place in North America (including the Mississippi).

Although many types of water craft have come down the Fraser River **through Hell's Gate**, only one has gone up the river here. It was the *Skuzzy* in 1862 and, according to some reports, it was "hauled through Hell's Gate by steam capstan and 125 men straining on ropes."

The **first sealing schooner** to arrive in B.C. was brought around the Horn, from Nova Scotia to Victoria, by Captain William O'Leary in the 1880s.

In 1886, Captain T.D. Shorts launched the Okanagan's **first steamer at Okanagan Landing.** Six years later, Okanagan Landing became a C.P.R. terminus and shipyard whose vessels made possible the growth of new towns and orchards in the valley. The Great War, new roads and railways, and the collapse of the fruit boom doomed the steamboats by 1916. In 1936, an era ended as the *Sicamous* steamed in from her last voyage.

The last sternwheeler in Canada to carry freight and passengers was the *SS Moyie*. Built in Nelson in 1898, she retired on April 27, 1957, completing almost 60 years of service on Kootenay Lake. The ship is now in drydock on the beach at Kaslo, and is the town's best known and biggest attraction. Through a huge, and successful, fund raising project, it is now undergoing an extensive program of restoration and repair. On board, the *Moyie* contains an enormous collection of artifacts and photographs depicting the area's history. It is well worth visiting. In 1978 the *S.S. Moyie* was designated a Historical Site by the Historic Sites and Monuments Board of Canada.

The *SS Samson V* was built in 1937 and is the **last steam powered paddlewheeler** in the Pacific Northwest. It is now a maritime museum in New West-

The "Beaver" on the rocks at Prospect Point, Stanley Park, Vancouver in 1988.

The sternwheeler "R.P. Rithet" at Yale in 1873

minster. It is also the fifth in the Samson class, the first one having entered service on the Fraser River in 1884.

The **first passenger ship** from the Soviet Union to visit Vancouver arrived on Feb. 26, 1977. It was the 20,000 ton *MS Mikhail Lermontov*, which was on a 64 day world cruise. The *Lermontov* is 176.8 m (580 ft.) long, has a beam of 23.5 m (77 ft.), a maximum speed of 21 knots, carries a crew of 350 and has a capacity for 600 passengers.

In 1986 the 350-ton ferry *Klatawa*, operating on the Fraser River between Albion and Fort Langley, became the **first passenger vessel in the world** to operate on a mixture of natural gas and diesel fuel.

Accidents at Sea

On November 4, 1875, the American steamer *Pacific*, leaving Victoria, **sank after a collision** off Cape Flattery at the entrance to Juan de Fuca Strait. There were two survivors. Loss of life was reported at 236 and bodies were washed ashore along a forty mile stretch of southern Vancouver Island.

In 1906, the U.S. steamer *Valencia* **crashed on the rocky coast** of Vancouver Island. Rough seas and rain hampered rescue operations. 126 perished.

The **biggest marine tragedy** in B.C.'s history occurred on the night of Oct. 24/25, 1918 when the Canadian Pacific passenger liner *Sophia* sank after striking Vanderbilt Reef. It was thought the ship would float free on the high tide and no attempt was made to take anybody off the vessel. A storm came up overnight and the seas were too turbulent to allow any rescue attempts, visibility was 100 m in the snow and the winds were blowing at 90 km/h. When it cleared in the morning, the ship was down with no survivors. A total of 343 men, women and children died in the wreck.

On May 22, 1971, at Vancouver B.C., the Norwegian cruise ship *Meteor* burned resulting in the loss of 32 lives.

The west coast of Vancouver Island is known to sailors as **"The Graveyard of the Pacific."** It received this title from the fact hundreds of ships have been wrecked on the reefs and rocks here in the last two hundred years or so.

Ports

New Westminster is believed to be the only Canadian city to have **paid for its wharves** with civic funds. They were built in 1912 and three years later, in 1915, with the completion of the Panama Canal, deep-sea vessels made this a major port of call.

There are **24 deep sea ports** along B.C.'s coast. Fifteen of these are within 120.7 km (75 mi.) of Vancouver.

Vancouver's waterfront covers 158 km (98 mi.) on Burrard Inlet. The port of Vancouver is the **largest bulk cargo port** on the Pacific coast of North America. It provides jobs for 57,000 workers.

Of the **top 10 ports in Canada**, British Columbia has one — the Port of Vancouver, and it is Canada's most active port in terms of volume — up to 30% of Canada's total.

Prince Rupert is the **third largest natural ice-free harbour** in the world.

Ferries

The British Columbia government lays claim to owning the **world's largest ferry system**. The B.C. Ferry Corp. began June 15, 1960 with two ships and two terminals. Today they are operating 38 ships on 25 routes. In their first year they carried 222,000 vehicles and 690,000 passengers. In the 1989/90 operating year they carried 7.5 million vehicles and 19.2 million passengers.

The **first car ferry**, the *Motor Princess* was built by the CPR in 1923 because of increasing automobile traffic. It was capable of carrying forty cars and ran between Vancouver and Nanaimo.

The B.C. Ferries Corporation operates **a larger fleet of ships** than the Canadian Navy. (B.C. Ferries: 38; Royal Canadian Navy: 32)

The ferry route (B.C. Ferries) between Tsawwassen, B.C., to Victoria, B.C., crosses the international border between Canada and the U.S. twice.

The Ministry of Transportation and Highways provides service on **17 freshwater routes**. This includes the Kootenay Lake ferry from Balfour to Kootenay Bay which is the longest free ferry ride in the world — about 45 minutes.

Lighthouses

The **first lighthouse** on the west coast is at Race Rocks, about 16 km (10 miles) west of Victoria. It was built of stone blocks of up to 1.8 m (6 ft.) thick, which were quarried and cut in Scotland and transported as ballast by ship around Cape Horn. It is B.C.'s southernmost lighthouse and is still in operation.

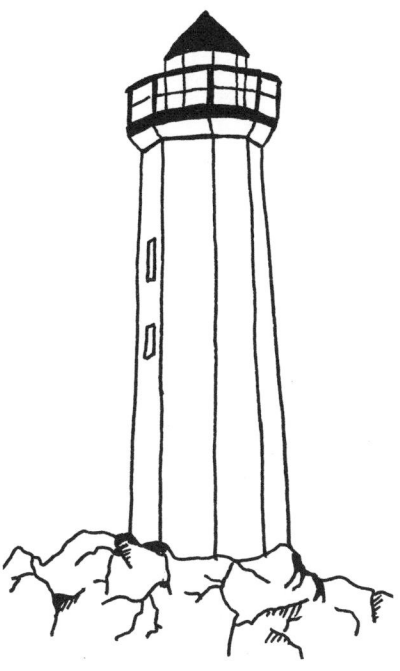

In 1910 a lighthouse was built on Triangle Island's highest point, making it the **most elevated primary lighthouse** in the world. The tower itself was only 14 m (46 ft.) high but it was located 213 m (700 ft.) above sea level. As this island was obscured by fog and low cloud for about half the year, the lighthouse was abandoned in 1924 in favor of nearby Cape Scott.

Fisgard Lighthouse was completed at the entrance to Esquimalt Harbour in 1861. Some claim it was the first lighthouse on the west coast to show a light.

Pachena Point Lighthouse was built in 1907 after one of the most disastrous shipwrecks in B.C. history, the wreck of the liner *Valencia*.

In 1911 there were **61 lighthouses** in operation in B.C. and four of these were on Kootenay Lake. There are now about **40 manned lighthouses** along B.C.'s coast. Other aids to coastal navigation in B.C. include about 480 buoys, 440 beacons, 950 lights, and 110 fog signals.

RAILWAYS

The **first railway in British Columbia** was a narrow-gauge railway between Seton and Anderson Lakes in 1860. It was three miles long and was powered by mules. Its rails were made of wood.

The **first dynamite blast** on the CPR's line in B.C. occurred at 9:00 a.m. May 15, 1880. The fuse was lit by Mr. R. Barry and was the beginning of No. 1 Tunnel just north of Yale.

Albert Rogers, credited with **discovering and surveying Roger's Pass** for the CPR in the 1880s, was given a cheque for

RIPPLE ROCK

One of the most dreaded obstacles to the marine navigator, Ripple Rock in Georgia Strait, was blown up on April 5, 1958. It has been estimated that since 1875 some 14 large ships and over 100 smaller vessels have sunk due to damage caused by this rock. Loss of life has been at least 114.

An attempt to blow it up in 1943, at a cost of over $1,000,000.00 was a complete failure. In 1955 work began on Maud Island. A 500-foot shaft was sunk and then a 2,370 ft. long tunnel was driven out to the rock. Two raises up its centre were stuffed with 2,750,000 lbs. of Nitramex 2H, which was specifically developed for this task.

A three mile danger zone was established around the area and at 9:33 a.m. April 5, 1958 the button was pushed. The resulting blast was the largest non-nuclear peacetime explosion in history. Thirty months to engineer, at a cost of $3,100,000.00, the top 350,000 tons of Ripple Rock were gone in a matter of seconds.

$5,000 for his work. He told CPR boss, William Van Horne he didn't do it for the money, but rather because he liked the challenge. He then framed the cheque.

A blasting accident on May 28, 1880 caused the death of William Flynn. He was the first fatality on the CPR line in B.C.

The **first CPR engine** in B.C. was barged in and placed on the section of track completed between Emory Bar and Yale on July 4, 1881.

The **first steel cantilever bridge** in North America was built in 1882 across the Fraser River near Lytton and was described as "one of the great wonders of the CP Railway."

On May 27, 1884 a government railway inspector **drove the first spike** in B.C. on the CPR line coming through the Kicking Horse Pass. The last spike, in the Northwest Territories (present-day Alberta), was driven by the wife of Superintendent F.P. Brothers.

The Canadian Pacific Railway was **completed "from coast to coast"** with the driving of the last spike at 9:22 a.m. on the 7th of November, 1885. The man with the hammer was Donald A. Smith (later to become Lord Strathcona). The location was 16.7 miles east of Sicamous, B.C. William Cornelius Van Horne, the railway's Vice-President in charge of construction, named the spot Craigellachie. At this time the western terminus of the CPR was Port Moody.

A C.P.R. train in the Fraser Canyon in 1884.

The **first passenger train of the CPR** from Montreal to Port Moody arrived July 4, 1886. It pulled into the station at exactly one minute past noon amid the cheers of thousands of people out to celebrate the event. At least a thousand people came by excursion boats from New Westminster, Victoria and Nanaimo.

The **first CNR train** arrived in Vancouver on Aug. 28, 1915.

The **first electric interurban public transit line** in North America was inaugurated in October of 1891. It was known as the Central Park Line of the Westminster and Vancouver Tramway Company.

During the period of Jan. 22nd to the 26th, 1935, the railway through Rogers Pass, B.C., was **blocked by avalanches** in at least 11 different places.

The arrival of the first C.P.R. transcontinental passenger train in Vancouver, 1887

British Columbia Railway Co., at Tumbler Ridge, B.C., began operating Canada's **first 50,000 volt electric railway** on Nov. 24, 1983.

On Nov. 7, 1985 the fourth Lord Strathcona **drove a symbolic spike** on the spot where his great grandfather, Donald Smith, the first Lord Strathcona, drove the last spike that completed the transcontinental CPR line one hundred years earlier. The ceremony, at Craigellachie, attracted over 1,000 people from all over the continent.

The Light Rapid Transit (LRT) system, on B.C.'s Lower Mainland, known as **Skytrain**, began operating on Jan. 3, 1986. The line at that time was from New Westminster to Vancouver and it was built at a cost of $854 million. It has since been extended across the Fraser River into Surrey. In its first year it carried 34 million passengers of which 6.6 million were Expo 86 passengers, travelling between the main Expo site and Canada Place in Vancouver.

Railway Facts

One of the **most famous railways in the world,** when it was built, was the White Pass & Yukon Railway. It was constructed in 1898-1900 and ran from Skagway, Alaska, to Whitehorse, Yukon. Along the way it went approximately 45 miles through British Columbia.

One of the **shortest railways in Canada** had one of the **highest fares**. It charged $2.00 in the year 1900 to go the full distance of $2\frac{1}{4}$ miles between Taku and Atlin Lake.

The **longest rail crossing over the Fraser River** is the CNR's Cisco Bridge. Located in the Fraser Canyon and built in 1912, it is 247.5 m (812 ft.) long and 67 m (220 ft.) above the water.

The **second transcontinental railway** in Canada, the Grand Trunk Pacific, was completed on April 7, 1914. The last spike was driven between Fraser Lake and Vanderhoof, B.C. (Approx. 135 km W of Prince George). In 1923 it was amalgamated into the Canadian National Railways system, which was formed in 1919.

For the 100th Anniversary of the driving of **"The Last Spike,"** CP Rail had Locomotive 1201 in attendance. It was the last steam locomotive built by CP's Angus Shops in Montreal and was basically a utility machine used for secondary mainline and branchline duties. It is now owned by the National Museum of Science and Technology, but was brought out as a crowd pleaser for this historic occasion.

British Columbia is served by two national railways, CPR and CNR, two provincial railways, BCR and BCHR, and one US railway, Burlington Northern. They have a combined total of about 7,500 km (4,660 mi.) of mainline track in B.C.

British Columbia Railway, (BCR), a **provincially operated railway** with 2,027 km (1,259 1/2 mi.) of track, is Canada's third largest railway.

The Pacific Great Eastern Railway was neither Pacific, great nor eastern. The railway was built in 1912 and ran out of money before it was completed. It was taken over by the provincial government in 1972 and renamed **BC Rail**.

The CPR's Trans-Canada Limited, refitted in 1929, was considered to be one of the **"Great Trains of the World."** The Railway Museum in Cranbrook has the only completely restored collection of this train including the dining car, sleeper, and baggage car.

The Macdonald Tunnel, on the CP Rail line in Rogers Pass, is the **longest railway tunnel** in North America. It is 14.66 km (9.1 mi.) in length and replaces the 8 km (4.9 mi.) Connaught Tunnel, which opened in 1916. The Macdonald Tunnel, officially opened May 4, 1989, is thought to be one of the most expensive sections of railway in the world at $15 million per kilometre.

Vancouver Bridge, Canada's **longest railway lift span**, connects Vancouver and North Vancouver over Burrard Inlet. It is in three sections, the longest being 150 m (493 ft.). The bridge is part of a project that includes a 2 mile tunnel on the Vancouver side.

The Royal Hudson is the **only steam locomotive** operating on any major railway line in North America, and is also the last surviving example of its class.

These are the first Skytrain tickets. They were bought in New Wesminster by Don Blake. The ticket was bought at 4:10 a.m. The return ticket was purchased at Waterfront Station in Vancouver at 5:55 a.m., both on Jan. 13, 1986.

A MONUMENT TO THE CHINESE

Located at the Yale Museum, in the Fraser Canyon, is a monument the likes of which there are very few in Canada. What makes it unique among the monuments put up by the Historic Sites and Monuments Board of Canada is the fact that it is trilingual — English, French and Chinese. It was put up as a tribute to the Chinese construction workers on the Pacific Railway. It reads as follows, in the three languages:

"In the early 1880s contractor Andrew Onderdonk brought thousands of labourers from China to help build the Pacific Railway through the mountains of British Columbia. About three-quarters of the men who worked on the section between the Pacific and Craigellachie were Chinese. Although considered excellent workers, they received only a dollar a day, half the pay of a white worker. Hundreds of Chinese died from accidents or illness, for the work was dangerous and living conditions poor. Those who remained in Canada when the railway was completed securely established the basis of British Columbia's Chinese community."

HIGHWAYS

"British Columbia is a land of scenic enchantments, but if it possessed no scenic attractions, no beauty spots to lure the travelling motorist, its splendid highways would still prove of sufficient attraction to draw the enthusiastic tourist to its enchanted gates." *Weigley's B.C. Directory, 1918*

History

The **first express service** in British Columbia started in the summer of 1858. Billy Ballou, with agents in San Francisco, Fort Victoria, New Westminster and Fort Yale, carried mail, newspapers and small parcels to the miners on the bars of the Fraser River. Where possible, he went by steamer or canoe but his main method of travel was by foot. His rates were $1.00 to $2.00 for letters depending on the destination, $1.00 for newspapers and a percentage of the value for parcels and packages with a minimum charge of $3.00.

About 1860, the Royal Engineers' Road from Hope to Princeton rose to a height of 1829 m (6000 ft.) thus making it one of the **highest passes** in Canadian highway history. Parts of this road still remain and can be seen along side of today's highway.

The **first road building** in British Columbia, of any major proportions, was the "Cariboo Wagon Road." It was constructed between 1862 and 1865 at a cost of $1,500,000. It was 6 m (18 ft.) wide and 640 km (400 mi.) long, and began at Yale, the head of steam navigation on the Fraser. The Caribou road aimed to secure all the trade for that river, thus excluding American competition. Intended to reduce the costs of goods in the mining area of the Caribou gold fields, and to encourage British immigrants and capitalists to come there, the road put the colony deeply into debt.

The **first wagon road** to be surveyed in B.C. was the Pavilion Mountain Road north of Lillooet. It was surveyed by Sgt. James McMurphy of the Royal Engineers and the road was completed in 1863.

"Cariboo" Cameron is believed to have made the **first bicycle** in B.C. and used it on trips from Barkerville to Quesnel and back. (Mr. Cameron is well known for his gold discoveries in the Cariboo) The bicycle he built and used is on display in the museum in Vancouver.

In 1899 the **first automobile** arrived in Vancouver. It was steam powered.

The **first taxi business** began in Vancouver in 1903.

Frank and Fred Begg started the **first automobile dealership** in British Columbia in 1904.

The **British Columbia Automobile Association** (BCAA) is Canada's largest automobile club. It was formed in Victoria as the Victoria Automobile Club in 1906. In 1962 the BCAA introduced the first emergency road service fleet of its kind in Canada. Now in its 85th year (in 1991), the BCAA has about 450,000 members in 16 service chapters throughout the province.

In 1908 Canada's **first gas station** opened at the Shell gasoline warehouse in Vancouver. Gasoline was pumped into cars through a garden hose.

The **first motor road** through the central Canadian Rockies was the Banff-Windermere Road. It was built by the federal government and completed in 1922.

The **first commercial driving school** in Canada was started in 1946 in Vancouver by William McKinley.

Mile "0" of the Caribou Wagon Road at Lillooet, B.C.

Transcontinental

In 1921 two Halifax residents named Burkman and Carr decided to try to **walk to Vancouver** via the railway line, just as an adventure. After they started out a middle-aged postman named John Behan and his 24-year-old son took out after them, followed two weeks later by Frank Dill and his wife Jennie. At that point Sid Carr said he was out for a walk, not a race, and he got on a train and went back to Halifax. The other five all made it to Vancouver — 5,793.5 km (3600 mi.) in six months. The postman and his son were there first.

A new record **cross-Canada walk**, along the Trans-Canada Highway from Halifax to Vancouver, was completed on Aug. 4, 1973. Clyde McRae, 23, left Halifax on May 1 and completed the 6,057 km (3,764 mi.) in 96 days.

The **first transcontinental motorist** arrived in Vancouver in early October, 1921. On August 20, 1921 Thomas Willey, of England, dipped the rear wheels of his automobile into the Atlantic Ocean at Halifax and set off the following day with the intention of dipping the front ones in the Pacific at Vancouver. He even carried a small bottle of Atlantic water which, he said, was to sweeten the Pacific. Even though he "cheated" by taking a train from North Bay, Ontario to Sudbury, Ontario, and a boat from Sault Ste. Marie to Port Arthur, he managed to arrive in Calgary in early September. From Calgary to Banff he was forced to winch his auto over some of the more difficult spots with a block and tackle, and from Cranbrook he had to ride the railway almost all the way across the mountains to Hope. His journey was accomplished at an average speed of almost 161 km (100 mi.) per day.

The Trans Canada Highway is **the longest paved road in the world**. It officially opened in 1962 and it measures 7821 km (4860 mi.) from Mile "0" at Beacon Hill Park in Victoria, B.C. to Signal Hill, St. Johns, Newfoundland. The B.C. section of the Trans Canada Highway (Hwy. No. 1), Victoria to the Alberta border is 993 km (617 mi.)

Accidents

The **first recorded death** from an automobile accident in B.C. was in 1913.

The **worst road accident** in B.C. history happened July 15, 1975. A head-on collision near Princeton caused the deaths of eleven persons, including a family of eight from Richmond.

A pickup truck **collided** with a lowbed semi-trailer on September 3, 1977 causing the trailer to cross the highway just as a bus was approaching. The resulting crash killed 10 people and injured 16 more. This occurred near Nanaimo and is the worst traffic accident on Vancouver Island and second-worst in B.C..

A story from the British Columbia Automobile Association in 1989 said B.C. drivers are the **worst in Canada** and they have "atrocious" habits. It also said the most common causes of accidents are: following too closely, running red lights, and failing to yield the right-of-way.

There are **more traffic accidents** at intersections than at any other place on the roads and highways of this province.

Seat belts are designed to protect a person in the event of a collision. Their effectiveness this way has been proven. There is another benefit to wearing seat belts, and that is that they actually help to prevent collisions from occurring. How? With a seat belt fastened, it is easier for the driver to control a vehicle in an emergency manoeuvre because it keeps him firmly planted behind the wheel.

The Law

On January 1, 1922, **a new law** came into effect in B.C. requiring motorists to drive on the right hand side of the road rather than on the left. The first motor vehicle accident after the new law was effected, and perhaps even on account of it, was a head-on collision between two cars, on a corner, one on the right hand side of the road and the other on the left. The driver of the one on the right (and in the right) was Claude Harvie, working for the Municipality of Surrey. He had been out most of the night changing and putting up the new road signs when the collision occurred. No one was injured and the other driver's name was not recorded.

Seat belts must be worn by all drivers and passengers of motor vehicles in British Columbia.

All persons riding on motorcycles in British Columbia must wear **safety helmets**.

If you need **highway or road reports** within B.C. call toll free, 24 hours, 1-800-663-4997.

In 1989 there were 1,394,000 licensed passenger vehicles and 491,000 licensed commercial vehicles in British Columbia.

The **only toll highway** in B.C. is the Coquihalla Highway and the toll station is about half way between Hope and Merritt. The fares vary according to vehicle type and/or size. For the average car the charge is ten dollars.

Parking meters in Vancouver contribute almost $6 million annually to the city's bank account. (Parking meters were invented by Carl Magee in Oklahoma City and the first one was put into service on July 16, 1935.

Roads

In the 1930s the road between Princeton and Coalmont with 292 curves in 19.3 km (12 miles) was called the **"most damnable highway in B.C."**

In British Columbia there are 21,905 kilometres of paved roads and 20,200 kilometres of unpaved roads.

There are about 150 km (93.2 mi.) of paved highway on the Queen Charlotte Islands and thousands of km of gravel logging road.

The **longest continuous hill** on any major roadway in Canada is the west side of the Creston/Salmo Highway (No.3). It is 23.5 km (14.6 mi.) uphill (going east) or downhill (going west). It is also Canada's 3rd highest all-weather mountain pass at 1,774 m (5,820 ft.). (The two highest passes are in Alberta.)

The highest point on the Yellowhead Highway, which runs from Winnipeg to Prince Rupert and to Kamloops, is not in B.C. at all but approximately 125 km (77.7 mi.) east of the B.C.-Alberta border at Obed Summit.

The Squamish Highway, between West Vancouver and Squamish, is called **"The Killer Highway"**. The worst section is between West Vancouver and Britannia Beach which Equinox Magazine says is "the 14 most dangerous miles of road in Canada". The problem here is the heavy rains which cause washouts and slides. About 50 people have died from these slides since the turn of the century. Eleven of those have died since 1980.

The highway with the **most road signs in B.C.** is between Horseshoe Bay and Squamish, approximately 44 km (27.3 mi). On one recent trip, on both sides of the road, I counted 740 signs.

The highway with **the least number of signs** is between Kitchener and Yahk in southeastern B.C., a distance of about 20 km. There are very few.

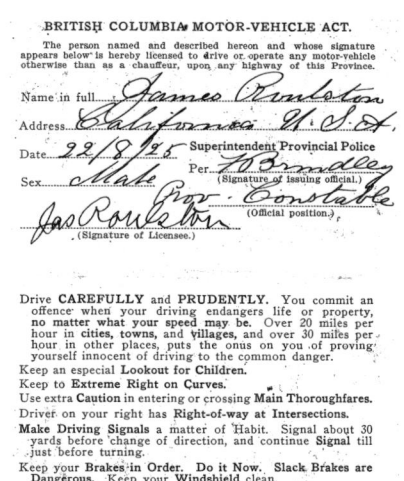

This British Columbia driver's licence was issued to Mr. James Roulston, whose address was, very simply, California, U.S.A., on August 25, 1922. Note the statement that the driver must prove himself innocent, rather than being innocent until proven guilty.

The municipality of Surrey is served by six major roads — #1, 1A, 10, 15, 99 and 99A. These roads connect to, or form a part of, the 1,200 km of roads in the municipality. They are also served by four railways and the Fraser/Surrey Docks which accommodates deep-sea vessels. Surrey's population (Est. 1991) is 250,000.

Bridges & Tunnels

The **Lion's Gate Bridge**, connecting Vancouver to North and West Vancouver, is the 20th longest suspension bridge in North America. It was built in 1939 and the longest span is 472.5 m (1550 ft.).

The **Deas Island Tunnel** was officially opened in July, 1959 by Queen Elizabeth. It is located on Hwy 99 between Vancouver and the international boundary. At the time it was built, it was the largest prefabricated tunnel in the world, and about 640 m (2100 ft.) of it is under the Fraser River at depths down to about 18 m (60 ft.). The name was later changed to the George Massey Tunnel.

The **longest steel arch bridge** in Canada, and 4th in length in North America is the Port Mann Bridge over the Fraser River. It was built in 1964 on the Trans Canada Highway connecting the municipalities of Surrey and Coquitlam. Its longest span is 366 m (1200 ft.) between the supports, and its total length, from end to end, is 2058.8 m (6754.6 ft.)

The opening of the **Cog Harrington Bridge** between Boston Bar and North Bend on January 28, 1986, marked the closing of the unique Aerial ferry which had been in use at this point since March 15, 1940. It had originally been installed at a cost of $20,000 and, at the time of closing, had annual operating costs of about $300,000. Construction of the bridge began in September 1983 and was completed at a cost of about $6 million.

The **Alex Fraser Bridge**, over the Fraser River between Annacis Island and North Delta, is the longest cable stayed bridge in the world and was built at a cost of $300 million. The south tower of the bridge is 154 m (500 ft.) high — the height of a 50-story building, making it the tallest man-made structure in B.C. It is 465 m (1,525 ft.) between the towers.

The **longest tunnel** on the Trans Canada Highway is the China Bar Tunnel in the Fraser Canyon between Yale and Boston Bar. Its length is 650 m (2,132 ft.).

The **longest snowshed** on the Trans-Canada Highway is in Rogers Pass. There are eight snowsheds in this area, the longest being about 600 m (1,968.5 ft.) in length

THE MEMORIAL

A Tree That Moved A Highway

The story of this tree's memorial status starts when the tree was about 300 years old. Winter Perkins settled and began farming this area in 1908. In the First World War, his son Charlie left to join the Royal Flying Corps. When the war was over Charlie returned and began to plant ivy around an old Douglas fir on his father's property, as a tribute to his fallen comrades. This was the last standing Douglas fir on his father's homestead. When the Department of Highways planned to put a freeway through the area, Charlie approached Highways Minister Phil Gaglardi and explained to him what the tree meant and it was agreed the highway, at that point, would have a "little kink" in it. The old ivy-covered Douglas Fir, which once stood 61 m (200 ft.) high, was cut down in 1968 as a safety measure.

ALASKA HIGHWAY

(From Dawson Creek B.C. to Fairbanks, Alaska)

After the bombing of Pearl Harbor in 1941, the American and Canadian governments agreed to jointly build road access into Alaska for the defence of the West Coast. Right-of-way was provided by Canada, which also waived import duties, sales and income taxes, and normal immigration processes. Canada also provided construction materials. The Americans paid for the project and provided the men and machinery required. Construction began in March 1942 and, at one point, about 30,000 American troops were working along its length. The project was completed in eight months and twelve days and the official opening was held at Soldier's Summit, Yukon, on Nov. 20, 1942.

Although it was officially completed in 1942, the Alaska Highway was far from finished. Reconstruction and upgrading programs were begun almost immediately and are still being carried out.

The Alaska Highway was originally called, and is still known, as the Alcan Highway. This is short for Alaska-Canada Military Highway. However it is very seldom referred to by this name today.

The Alaska Highway today is considered to be more of a road through the wilderness than a wilderness road (as it originally was). The highway is gradually being shortened by reconstruction and upgrading.

Control of the Canadian section of the Alaska Highway was turned over to the Canadian Government at the end of the Second World War, and the highway was opened to the public in 1948.

Within B.C. the Alaska Highway is Highway No. 97, within the Yukon it is No. 1, and within Alaska it is No. 2.

The highest point on the Alaska Highway is at Summit Lake, B.C. — 1295 m (4,250 ft.) at Mile 392.

The Alaska Highway crosses the B.C.–Yukon border five times.

AIRWAYS

History

Canada's **first aviation fatality** was Charles Marble. He died shortly after being pulled out of the Fraser River at New Westminster after his balloon malfunctioned and crashed. This was on October 10, 1894 during the Royal City Fair.

On September 8, 1910 Mr. W.W. Gibson made the first airplane flight in British Columbia, near Victoria. He built the plane himself including the six-cylinder engine which powered it.

The second flight, and the first on the mainland, took place shortly after at Minoru Park race track in Richmond in front of a crowd of 3500. The pilot was Charles Hamilton and he flew a Curtiss biplane.

According to the 1989 Canadian Weather Calendar the "**first parachute jump** in Canada was made by Charles Saunders in Vancouver" on May 24, 1912.

MOUNTAIN PASSES

There are 14 mountain passes on B.C. roads:

Allison	1,342 m	(4,403 ft.)
Monashee	1,189 m	(3,901 ft.)
Bonanza	1,535 m	(5,036 ft.)
Pine	933 m	(3,061 ft.)
Coquihalla	1,245 m	(4,085 ft.)
Rogers	1,327 m	(4,354 ft.)
Crowsnest	1,396 m	(4,580 ft.)
Sinclair	1,486 m	(4,875 ft.)
Heckman	1,524 m	(5,000 ft.)
Summit	1,219 m	(3,999 ft.)
Kicking Horse	1,643 m	(5,390 ft.)
Vermilion	1,640 m	(5,381 ft.)
Kootenay	1,774 m	(5,820 ft.)
Yellowhead	1,066 m	(3,497 ft.)

In 1912 Olive Stark, on a brief flight out of Vancouver, became the **first female airplane passenger** in Canada.

The first flight to be made by a **female pilot** in Canada was in a Curtiss biplane, piloted by Mrs. Alys McKey at Vancouver on July 31, 1913.

William Boeing established the **first international mail service** in North America, in 1919, flying a postal run between Vancouver and Seattle.

Also in 1919, the **first commercial air freight service** in B.C. was flown by George Trim between Vancouver and Victoria.

Cross country air service in Canada had its beginnings in the fall of 1920 when the newly formed Canadian Air Force ("Royal" was not added until April 1, 1924) ran a relay of at least three different planes from Halifax to Vancouver. It took 11 days with total airtime of 45 hours.

Completing the **first seaplane flight** ever made across North America and the first airplane flight ever made across Canada, Squadron Leader A. Earl Godfrey of the Royal Canadian Air Force arrived at Jericho Beach September 19, 1926 at 4:20 p.m. His Douglas seaplane took off from Montreal September 12th and the transcontinental trip was concluded after several delays of bad weather.

In 1928 B.C. Airways began the **first regularly scheduled passenger service** in the province, between Vancouver, Victoria and Seattle.

This must be one of the most photographed road signs in the world: the Mile "0" marker for the Alaska Highway. It is one of two located in Dawson Creek, one at the present starting point and this one a couple of blocks away at the original starting point.

The **first major airline** to operate international flights from B.C. was United Airlines. On July 1, 1934 it began a service from Vancouver to Seattle on a trial basis. This experiment was tremendously successful and scheduled flights soon began.

PILOT'S LICENCES

The following pilot's licences are in forcei B.C. as of Oct. 1, 1991:

Private Pilot	4841
Commercial	1588
Senior Commercial	177
Airline Transport	703
Private Helicopter	4
Commercial Helicopter	648
Airline Transport Helicopter	164
Glider	693
Gyroplane	3
Free Balloon	20
Private Ultra-light	262
Commercial Ultra-light	166

Air Canada, under the name Trans-Canada Air Lines (TCA), began a **daily service**, Vancouver to Seattle, on September 1, 1937.

The world's **first trans-polar flight** was completed from Moscow to Vancouver in 1937.

Canadian Pacific Air Lines had its beginning in 1937 as Yukon Southern Air Transport owned by Grant McConachie. It operated from Vancouver to Prince George, Fort St. John, Fort Nelson and Whitehorse. (CPA did not come into existence, as such, until 1942.)

Scheduled passenger service by air was inaugurated from Montreal to Vancouver on April 1, 1939, and in 1941 it was extended to Halifax.

During World War II the Queen Charlotte Islands were the site of many **logging operations** to fill the need for spruce with the quality required for airplane construction.

Canadian Pacific Air Lines inaugurated the **first polar air service**, Vancouver to Amsterdam, in 1955.

Two Vancouver men set a new record for an **around-the-world flight** on commercial airlines. David Shore and Roger Matheson, C.P. Air passenger agents, left Los Angeles Thursday, December 1, 1977 and returned December 3, 1977 after stops at Frankfurt, Singapore and Sydney, Australia. The total elapsed time was 63 hours, 8 minutes and the total flying time was 43 hours, 10 minutes.

The previous record was 65 hours, 58 minutes. As airline employees they received reduced rates and the whole trip cost them $90.00 each. Application was made and accepted by the Guinness Book of World Records and it was recorded in the 1979 edition.

Accidents

The **first aircraft fatality** in Canada occurred in B.C. on August 6, 1913 when John Bryant was killed in Victoria.

The **worst airplane disaster in history** was on March 27, 1977. A KLM Royal Dutch Air Lines 747 collided on take-off with a Pan American Airways 747 at the Santa Cruz De Tenerife Airport on the Canary Islands. The death toll was 579. Most of the passengers were from the United States. Five were Canadian and four of these from B.C. The only Canadian survivor was Roy Tanemura of Kelowna. Mrs. Tanemura and Mr. and Mrs. Walter Mitchell, also of Kelowna, died in the crash.

Airports

Jericho Beach, at Vancouver, was selected as the **first air station** in B.C. In 1919 Earl L. MacLeod, of Sardis, helped select the site and he flew out of it for many years. He went on to command it as an R.C.A.F. station during the Second World War.

In 1929 Charles Lindbergh **declined to visit Vancouver** because the city lacked "an airport fit to land on." This incident is credited with persuading the city to invest in a municipal airport. Sea Island was selected, 190 hectares of land were acquired and in September, 1930 a foundation stone was laid for a solid brick administration building. The Vancouver Airport was officially opened July 22, 1931 by Premier S.F. Tolmie. (It did not become Vancouver International Airport until 1948.)

The popularity of Expo helped establish Vancouver International Airport as **the busiest airport** in the country in 1986. Transport Canada recorded 347,058 aircraft movements, an increase of 17 percent from 1985. Some 8,385,356 passengers used the airport, a 19.7 percent jump from 1985.

The **largest airport in British Columbia** is the Vancouver International Airport. The second largest is at Prince George.

The **third busiest airport** in B.C. is the Kelowna Airport. It is also a 24 hour customs point of entry.

In British Columbia there are 200 land-based airports, 63 water-based airports and 23 heliports. (This does not include any private facilities.)

B.C. is served by at least ten international airlines.

THE 1st AIR CROSSING

The first air crossing of the Canadian Rockies was on August 7, 1919. The following is from a plaque in the main terminal building of Vancouver International Airport:

"On August 7, 1919, Captain E.C. Hoy made the first crossing of the Canadian Rockies by air from Vancouver following a route over Vernon, Grand Forks, Cranbrook, and through Crawford Pass. His Canadian-built Curtiss JN-4 ("Jenny"), its flying altitude limited to 7,000 feet by an extra fuel load, took off from old Minoru Park Race Track, Lulu Island at 4:14 a.m. After manoeuvring between towering peaks and barely clearing heights of land en route, Hoy ended the history-making part of his flight at Lethbridge at 6:22 p.m. The hazards now behind him, he flew on to Calgary, landing at 8:55 p.m."

After reading this plaque and thinking about it for some time I came to the conclusion that by Crawford Pass, the writer probably meant Crowsnest Pass. I wrote to the National Historic Parks and Sites Branch in Ottawa and they responded that "... your suppositions appear to be correct." This plaque was originally put up at Galt Gardens Park in Lethbridge in the early 1960s and ten years later duplicated for Vancouver. The branch also said " . . . puzzling is the fact that a plaque has stood at Lethbridge for almost two decades, and another for half that time at Vancouver, both containing the same error, and no one has caught it till now . . . the error will, I am sure, be put right in due course."

Update: I recorded the above story in my 1985 book *This Is Beautiful British Columbia*, and again in my 1990 book *The Trivia Book of Alberta*. During 1991 I had the opportunity to visit both Lethbridge and Vancouver. The old plaques are still there, unaltered and incorrect.

On the top of the Granville Square building, in downtown Vancouver, is the **Harbour Control Tower**. Here air traffic controllers direct seaplane movements in and around Vancouver Harbour and other aircraft over the City of Vancouver. This control tower, at a height of 170 m (560 ft.) is the highest in North America and possibly the highest in the world.

◆

Dolores Schmidt was the **first female tower chief** (air traffic controller) in Canada. She became tower chief on December 19, 1983 at Langley after working at her trade for 22 years at Vancouver, Victoria and Abbotsford.

Odds & Ends

The **largest helicopter operating company** in Canada, and third largest in the world, is Okanagan Helicopters Ltd. of Vancouver. They have 110 helicopters and 500 employees.

◆

Earl Zilke, an airport worker at Prince George, was moving to a new apartment he found he didn't have room for "Ralph," his giant teddy bear. He took him to work where co-workers "adopted" him, put him in coveralls, and, with a tag around his neck saying "he wanted to see the world but be back in time for school," he was loaded on a plane July 28, 1988. On Sept. 4, 1988 he came back after "freeloading his way through eleven countries aboard twelve airlines" through most of the major centres of the world, and returned with several flight bags of gifts from all over the world.

◆

The Abbotsford International Airshow is one of the **top airshows** in the world and is held annually in August.

◆

One of the **largest producers of aerial forest fire fighting technology** in the world is Conair Aviation Ltd. of Abbotsford. The systems it has developed are in use in Australia, France, Italy, Japan, Portugal, Spain, and the United States.

◆

The British Columbia Aviation Council, an organization which promotes the development of aviation in the province, distributes maps and information on some 374 land and water aerodromes within its jurisdiction. For more information, phone (604) 278-9330.

MAJOR AIRLINE DISASTERS IN B.C.

Date	Aircraft Type	Location	No. Killed
Dec. 9, 1956	TCA *North Star*	Mt. Slesse near Chilliwack	62
July 8, 1965	CPA *DC6B*	100 Mile House	52
Feb. 11, 1978	PWA *737*	Cranbrook Airport	43
July 21, 1951	CPA *DC4*	Alaska-Korean Airlift	38
	DC4	near Sandspit QCI	36
Oct. 17, 1951	QCA *Canso*	Mt. Benson near Nanaimo	23
April, 1947	TCA *Lodestar*	near Sea Island Airport	15
June, 1957	PWA *DC3*	Port Hardy Airport	14
	CPA	Mt. Cheam near Chilliwack	13
Nov. 24, 1952	RCAF	Comox	12

One other incident which is not generally considered a B.C. crash was that of a chartered Northwest Airlines DC7 on June 3, 1963. It crashed into the Pacific off the B.C. coast with the loss of 101 lives.

CHAPTER 7

BUSINESS & INDUSTRY

FORESTRY

History

The **first sawmill** in British Columbia was set up at Millstream (near Victoria) in 1848.

The **first "forest industry" strike** in B.C. was by axemen working for the British Boundary Commission. They went on strike for higher wages in June of 1859.

When the **Willows Hotel**, in Campbell River, opened for business in 1909, the barroom had a bar with a top which was a single slab of fir 12.2 m long by 45.7 cm wide by 7.6 cm thick (40 ft. x 18 in. x 3 in.).

The **first paper made in B.C.** was at the B.C. Pulp and Paper Manufacturing Co. located on the Somass River at Port Alberni. Production began in July 1894 but the mill was forced to shut down in 1896 due to a shortage of rags. (Rags were the main ingredient of paper at that time as their machinery would not produce a satisfactory product from wood pulp.)

During the late '20s and early '30s the Abernathy Lougheed Logging Company was considered to be one of the **largest logging companies** in the world. It was located in the Maple Ridge area and employed between 700 and 800 men in 8 camps in and around Alouette Lake. This is now Golden Ears Provincial Park.

A ceremony held in Stanley Park, Vancouver, in 1930, saw the planting of a seedling to mark the birth of the **Junior Forest Wardens** in Canada. The seedling was a Douglas Fir which is today a growing symbol of the success of the organization. Their goal was to educate

This "Tree Crusher" at MacKenzie is big! It is 17m long, 6.5m high, 10.7m wide, weighs 158,760 kg and has a top speed of 4.8 km per hour.

young people and, through them, reach their parents about the dangers of fire. Since then, their objectives have expanded to "cover a wide range of forest ecology" and the forest environment.

Forestry Facts

Forestry is the **most important primary industry** in B.C. Almost a quarter of a million people in the province depend on forestry either directly or indirectly.

The government of B.C. owns **94% of the province's forest land**, private interests own 5% and the federal government the rest. Forest based industries directly employ about 7% of B.C.'s work force. The silviculture program sees about 200 million seedlings planted annually which replaces about 60% of the areas harvested, the remainder being treated for natural regeneration.

Productive forest land in British Columbia **covers about 43.3 million hectares** or 46% of the province. Approximately

---

NOTICE

by T.F. Daly, Superintendent, Bloedel, Stewart & Welch Ltd. Bloedel, B.C. March 31, 1941:

"The practice of pissing around the bunkhouses must be stopped. If this practice is not discontinued, during the summer months there will be such a stink around the bunkhouses that men cannot live there. You men living in the bunkhouses should make it your business to see that this practice is stopped, not alone for your own welfare, but the sanitary conditions of the whole camp. The water closet is such a short distance from the bunkhouses there is no occasion for a man pissing off the steps of the bunkhouse, and when I ask that this practice be stopped, I mean it."

The Elk Falls Mill of Crown Forest Products in Campbell River.

96% of this is coniferous, which means B.C. has about half of the total softwood inventory in Canada.

British Columbia's coastal areas contain about **2 percent of Canada's forest** area and supplies almost 25 percent of the total wood cut. The main species are Western Redcedar, Hemlock, Spruce, Fir and Douglas Fir.

British Columbia produces approximately 85% of Canada's softwood plywood, 62% of Canada's softwood lumber, 30% of Canada's pulp and 17% of Canada's paper.

B.C.'s forestry industry operates on the principal of sustained yield with the slogan **"Forests Forever."**

British Columbia's forest product exports have a value of almost $10,000,000,000.00

Many of the **deep-sea freighters** clearing B.C. ports today carry enough lumber to build over one thousand average homes. By weight, lumber exports are second only to grain.

There are **24 pulp and paper mills** in B.C.

Log production in B.C. averages between 70 and 80 million cubic metres annually.

The Prince George area of B.C. is the **largest pulp producing area** in Canada.

There are about **50 types of trees** native to British Columbia (the exact number depends upon where the line is drawn between trees and shrubs).

There are literally hundreds of insects and diseases which affect all plant and tree life in the forests of British Columbia. Approximately 16 million cubic metres of wood is destroyed annually by insects and disease. **The worst** of these is the Dwarf Mistletoe, a parasitic plant, which accounts for about a third of this total loss.

The Douglas Fir was named after David Douglas in 1826 when he discovered this species of tree in the now State of Washington. In 1827, he moved to B.C. and may be considered B.C.'s first botanist.

It was reported in 1989 that a UBC graduate student had discovered a way to grow **square trees.**

The **second largest evergreen nursery** in Canada is located in Surrey, B.C.

Near the Village of Port Clements, Queen Charlotte Islands, is an attraction which many people have gone out of their way to see. It is the famous **Golden Spruce tree.** (As I understand it, it is somewhat of an oddity in the world of spruce trees).

British Columbia has **the biggest forests** with the biggest trees in Canada, and yet, there are parts of B.C. that are so dry trees will not grow there.

An **average size tree** in B.C. consumes approximately 270 L (60 gals.) of water per day. By coincidence this is also the same amount of water the average person uses per day.

The average tree produces 453,000 toothpicks.

The **weight of trees** per hectare in British Columbia's coastal forest is more than anywhere else in the world.

The Willows Hotel in Campbell River.

Records

What is believed to be the **world's largest burl** was recovered by MacMillan Bloedel loggers near Port McNeill on Vancouver Island. The giant spruce growth weighs 22.5 t and measures 13.7 m (45 ft.) in circumference.

The world's **largest logging sports show** takes place annually at the Pacific National Exhibition in Vancouver.

The **tallest known tree** in Canada is the 95 m (312 ft). tall "Carmanah Giant," a Sitka Spruce tree located in the Carmanah Valley on the southside of Vancouver Island. It was discovered in 1988 by Gordon Eason and Dennis Bendickson.

A **Douglas Fir tree** cut down in Lynn Valley in 1902 measured 126.5 m (415 ft.) in height.

The **largest Douglas Fir tree** in Canada has a circumference of over 12.5 m (41 ft.) at its base.

The **oldest Douglas Fir tree** in Canada grew on Vancouver Island. When cut down it was determined to have been over 1,300 years old.

At approximately 319 km (198 mi). north of the Yellowhead Highway, on the Cassiar Highway (No. 37), is the Iskut Burn where fire destroyed 31,580 ha (78,000 acres) in 1958. After the fire the area turned into British Columbia's **largest huckleberry patch**.

The "Entwined Tree" at Midway.

Tree-ring dating expert Marion Parker discovered what is believed to be the **oldest tree stump** in Canada. The tree was a yellow cedar and checked out at 1,636 years old. It was discovered in B.C.'s "Sunshine Coast" area.

The **largest stand of redwood trees** north of California is in Surrey, B.C. at Redwood Park.

The **tallest flagpole** in the world is standing in the Royal Botanical Gardens, London, England. It is a 371-year old Douglas Fir which stands 82 m (270 ft.) tall. It was cut in 1958 by the B.C. Coast Forest Industries and sent as a centennial gift. It came from MacMillan Bloedel's Copper Canyon camp on Vancouver Island.

The **largest tree ever shipped by rail** became the tallest flagpole in Canada. It was a 300 year old Douglas Fir with a length of 56.4 m (185 ft.). It came from Rithet Creek in the Sooke Lake area of Vancouver Island. Three flatdeck cars were used to transport it to the Canadian National Exhibition grounds in Toronto, November 1976.

TOTEM POLES

The **totem pole** has become a symbol of B.C. known around the world. Originally they were status symbols among B.C.'s six coastal tribes.

The **tallest totem pole** in the world is 52.7 m (173 ft.) tall. It was raised on June 6, 1973, at Alert Bay, Vancouver Island, B.C. It tells the story of the Kwakiutl and it took 36 man-weeks to carve. Previous to this the world's tallest totem pole was 38.9 m (127 ft. 7 in.), carved and erected in 1956 in Beacon Hill Park, Victoria.

One of the **largest outdoor collections** of totem poles in B.C. is at Prince Rupert. Being at the geographical centre of the Haida and Tsimpsian tribes, the poles of these two peoples are accessible by a circular "Walking Tour" in the downtown area of Prince Rupert.

The Upper Skeena is also renowned for its claim as the **"Totem Pole Capital of the World."** Nowhere else on Earth can visitors see so many original totems standing where they were first erected in the 1800s.

MINING

History

Archaeologists say British Columbia's **mineral industry** had its beginnings about 9,000 years ago. A recent "dig" near Yale showed B.C.'s earliest known inhabitants made use of natural mineral materials such as basalt, jade, native copper, obsidian, sandstone, serpentine, silica (quartz), slates and soapstones.

The **first mine in B.C.** was a coal mine opened in 1835. The mine was at Fort Rupert at the north end of Vancouver Island. It was owned and operated by the Hudson's Bay Company.

The Bluebell Mine at Riondel on Kootenay Lake, was **B.C.'s first lode mine**. Although it was not staked until either 1878 or 1883 (depending on which Minister of Mines Reports you are reading), it was known long before then. In its 76 year history as a producing mine (it shut down in 1971), it produced 5,313,201 tons of ore containing 548,667,827 pounds zinc, 515,300,410 pounds lead, 7,130,889 ounces silver, 6,294,950 ounces copper, and 285 ounces gold. *(Figures courtesy of Cominco Ltd.)*

During 1896 there were at least **55 operating mines** shipping high grade silver ore from the Slocan area.

On Feb. 18, 1965 an **avalanche killed 26 workmen** and injured 20 others on Granduc Mountain near Stewart, B.C. where the Granduc mine was being developed. Prior to the avalanche, a great storm raged for several days dropping an estimated 4.3 m (14 ft.) of snow on the surrounding mountains.

At the Rossland Historical Museum the restoration of the "Miner's Union Hall" has been completed. This hall is thought to be the home of the **first industrial labor union** in Canada. It was built in 1898.

In the 1930s, the copper mines at Britannia Beach near Vancouver were the **largest copper producers** in the British Empire. In the seventy year period from 1904 to 1974, 1.3 billion pounds of copper was extracted. The B.C. Museum of Mining, which opened its doors in May of 1975, keeps the memory alive with an underground train ride, displays of historic hard rock mining equipment, and an outstanding display called "Britannia: the story of a British Columbia Mine."

Mining Facts

The Bralorne-Pioneer Mine, at Bralorne, B.C., produced over four million ounces of gold and 1.2 million ounces of silver during its seventy years of operation. This mine resulted from the merger of the Bralorne Mine and the Pioneer Mine.

The value of mineral production in British Columbia in 1989 was $4.2 billion.

Coal was the province's **most valuable mineral product** in 1989. It made up 25% of the province's mineral production and had a value of $1.04 billion.

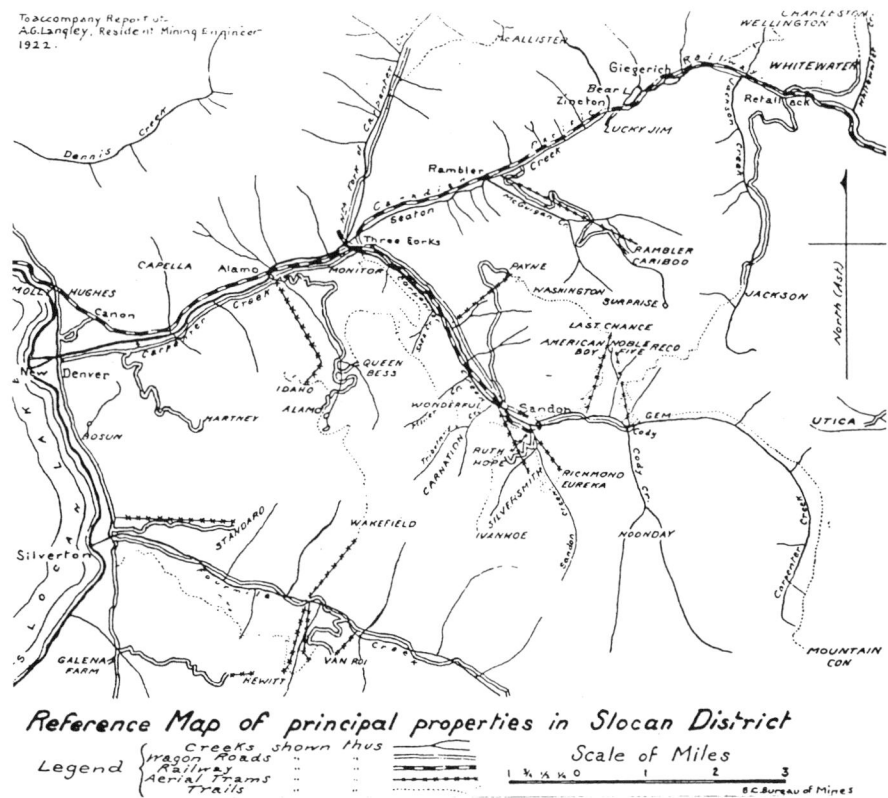

This 1922 Reference Map shows some of the mining properties in the Slocan area. Courtesy of the Minister of Mines Report, B.C. Dept. of Mines.

Metals accounted for **42.8% of the province's mineral** production in 1989. Copper was at the head of this list with a value of $1.006 billion.

Today there are only about twenty hard rock mines and six coal mines in all of B.C.

The **only hard rock gold mine** in Canada, open to the public, is the Le Roi Mine located at Rossland, B.C.

The **underwater lands** of B.C.'s coast, inside and outside of the islands, contain extensive deposits of mineable ores of commercial grades.

The **first aluminum plant** in Western Canada was in New Westminster. The B.C. Aluminium Co. cast its first bar of pure aluminum in November, 1951.

At the same time, construction was going ahead on Alcan's (Aluminum Co. of Canada) smelter at Kitimat which ultimately became, and still is, one of the **largest aluminum smelters** in the world.

Kitimat Works imports aluminum oxide (unprocessed aluminum) from Australia, Jamaica and Japan, producing more than 270,000 t of aluminum every year.

Much of the world's **high grade chrysolite asbestos** comes from Cassiar, B.C.

The lustrous black stone known as "**argillite**," from which miniature to-

This monument to the Northwest Miner is in the Hazelton area and celebrates the first non-Indian settlers who came following the lure of gold and silver.

tems, earrings and pendants are carved, comes from a large deposit on the Queen Charlotte Islands. This deposit is protected by law and can be worked only by the Haida Indians

The Endako Mine near Fraser Lake, B.C., began production in 1965 and was the **largest producer of molybdenum** in Canada until 1982. (B.C. produces over 90% of Canada's molybdenum).

The lead/zinc smelter at Trail, B.C., produces about **5% of the world's supply** of these two metals.

Records

The **largest gold nugget** ever found in B.C., and possibly in Canada, was found in the Atlin area in July of 1987. It weighed in at 81 ounces with a gold value of about $40,000 and a collector's value of up to $75,000. Previous to this discovery the record was 72 ounces and it stood for 110 years. It was discovered by Alfred Freeman near Centreville, B.C., in the Cassiar District, 1877. (The Atlin Claim Newspaper contained an article in its 1991 Summer edition about a nugget weighing slightly over 83 ounces called the West Nugget that had been found in the area on July 12, 1899)

The **largest open pit coal mine** in Canada is at Sparwood, B.C. It is operated by Weston Mining Ltd. Their equipment includes the Terex Titan, the largest dump truck ever manufactured. (The Terex Titan is in the *Guinness Book of World Records*).

The Sullivan Mine at Kimberley is one of the **world's largest producers of lead-zinc-silver ores**. It came into production about 1910 and has since produced over 140 million tons of ore. This mine is the main feeder of the metallurgical complex at Trail.

The **largest primary producer of silver** in Canada is the Equity Silver Mine near Houston, B.C.

MAJOR MINE DISASTERS IN B.C.

Date	Place	Dead
May 3, 1887	No. 1 pit, Esplanade, Nanaimo	148
May 22, 1902	No. 2 colliery, Coal Creek, Fernie	125
Jan. 24, 1888	No. 5 pit, Wellington colliery	77
Feb. 15, 1901	No. 6 shaft, Union colliery	64
Aug. 13, 1930	No. 4 mine, Coalmont Collieries, Blakeburn	45

Oil & Gas

The northeast corner of British Columbia has the **only sedimentary basin** from which oil and gas is being produced.

A **natural gas field** in northeastern B.C. was discovered in 1989 and it is reported to be the most active field in Western Canada. It is located on the B.C.-Alberta border (80% in B.C.) approximately 160 km north of Fort St. John, B.C.

A **major natural gas field** has been discovered 40.2 km (25 mi). east of Fort St. John, B.C. The Boundary Lake field has reserves estimated at 200 billion cubic feet worth an estimated $100 million at current prices.

The Border-Ring field, the **newest major discovery of natural gas**, is estimated to contain recoverable reserves of one tcf (trillion cubic feet) of gas, worth over one billion dollars.

One of the **largest natural gas processing plants** in North America is at Fort Nelson, B.C.

The **largest oil refinery in B.C.** is Imperial Oil's 40,000 barrels-per-day plant at Ioco, near Port Moody.

There are over **12,000 km** (7,457 mi.) of oil and gas transmission lines in B.C.

GEOLOGICAL PHENOMENA

Earthquakes

British Columbia is the **most active earthquake area** in Canada with almost 200 recorded occurrences per year. Southwestern B.C. followed by the coastal areas have the highest number of recorded earthquakes, most of which are not even felt by the average person.

There are measurable **earthquakes every day** along the Pacific Rim but very few of them are actually "felt" without instruments.

Since 1899 British Columbia has had **over 40 earthquakes** that registered 6.0 or higher on the Richter Scale, and at least two registered 8.0.

The **first recorded earthquake** in B.C. occurred in the Fort Langley area on November 23, 1827.

The **strongest quake** in Canadian history occured off the Queen Charlotte Islands in 1949. It measured 8.0 on the Richter scale.

The **biggest recorded earthquake** to hit the Vancouver area registered 7.3 on the Richter Scale on June 23, 1946.

On March 30, 1964 a severe earthquake centered near Anchorage produced a **tidal wave** which caused heavy damage to communities along the west coast of Vancouver Island and northern Washington.

A minor earthquake on the morning of January 9, 1965 set off an enormous landslide on the Hope-Princeton Highway. More than 46 million cubic metres of earth, rock and snow came down in a matter of seconds, completely burying Outram Lake and wiping out about 3 kilometres of highway. Four people in three vehicles were killed, and two of the victims have never been found. This is the **largest recorded earth and rock slide** in B.C.

The Hope Slide Viewpoint.

Hot Springs

There are **95 known hot springs** in British Columbia.

Fairmont Hot Springs Tri-pool is Canada's **largest hot springs pool**. This unique pool goes through one million gallons of odorless mineral water per day. The resort has been called Canada's largest and finest "four season" resort and it is located in B.C.'s East Kootenay District.

Fairmont Hot Springs was originally developed in 1922 as a stagecoach stop on the road from Cranbrook to Golden. Today it is the **most popular year round resort** on the western side of the Canadian Rockies with over 750,000 visitors each year.

Harrison Hot Springs was discovered by accident during a winter storm when a small boat, carrying two prospectors, capsized, and threw its occupants into a pool of warm water.

Volcanos

On May 18, 1980, Mt. St. Helens spread a thin ash layer fell in the Okanagan Valley.

It is pretty well agreed by volcanologists that the **volcano most likely to erupt**, or potentially the most dangerous volcano in B.C., is Mount Meager, 2,679 m high, and approx. 150 km north of Vancouver in the Garibaldi Mountains. This danger is very slight and it last erupted about the year 360 B.C.

It is believed the **last volcanic eruption** to occur in Canada was about 200 years ago near Terrace, B.C.

At the Liard Hot Springs, Alpha pool, the temperature is 49°C (129°F). Beta pool, a little further up the trail is cooler at 38°C (100°F). These pools have been left in their natural state.

GEOLOGIC ODDITIES

Magnetic Hill, Vernon, B.C. —To find this geological oddity go up the Silver Star Road to Tillicum Road and to the Tillstar Campground gate. From here it is 3.2 km (2 mi.) via Tillicum Road and Dixon Dam Road. Go under the power lines and then uphill to a corner with seven birch trees. Stop at the second birch tree, put your car in neutral, and you should be able to feel the pull of the Earth's magnetic force.

The **world's largest "Jelly Roll,"** a fascinating geological formation, is found near Lytton, B.C.

The **Dutch Creek Hoodoos**, the result of the glaciation of the last ice age are worth a stop if you are in the area. Dutch Creek is only a couple of kilometres west of Fairmont Hot Springs.

FISHING

Point of Interest road sign at Moricetown, B.C.:"This site, **once the largest village of the Bulkley Valley Indians**, later was named after the pioneer Missionary, Father Morice. Salmon, staple food of the Indian, concentrated in the canyon and were caught with basketry traps, dipnets, and harpoons. Indians still catch salmon with long gaff hooks and smoke them at their historic native fishery."

(The above item is included in this section, because to the early Indians, it was definitely an industrial process necessary to their survival.)

There are about **78,000 commercial fishermen** in Canada; of these, about 67% are located on the Atlantic Coast, 25% on the Pacific Coast, and the remainder in the inland fisheries.

British Columbia's **fishing industry** in 1989 produced a wholesale value of about $886 million. This included salmon (592), Herring (147), Groundfish (69), Shellfish (51), and Halibut (27). *(Figures in brackets are millions of dollars.)*

In 1989 there were **20,578 valid commercial fishing licences** in British Columbia. It is estimated a little less than 16,000 of these are active.

There are over **forty species of fish** and marine animals being harvested and marketed by British Columbia's fishing and aquaculture industry.

Salmon is by far the **most valuable marine species** of B.C.'s commercial fishing industry, accounting for about 70% of the industry's wholesale value.

Exports of canned salmon from B.C. began in 1870. Today it is exported to almost 30 countries around the world.

The **oldest surviving cannery** in B.C. is the North Pacific Cannery at Port Edward, near Prince Rupert. It was built in 1889 and was one of nineteen canneries operating at the mouth of the Skeena River. It is now the only museum of its kind in B.C.

One of the **major spawning grounds** for Sockeye Salmon is the Adams River. During September and October, it is one of B.C.'s major attractions. During this period about 250,000 salmon fight their way up to their place of birth where the females lay their eggs and the males fertilize them. Then they both die. Every fourth year is a peak year when this figure rises to about a million. The next one will be in 1994.

The **world's largest salmon hatchery** is at Babine Lake.

The **mainstay of the West Coast fishing industry** are the five main species of salmon. The industry was established near the mouths of most rivers in the early days at the turn of the century, but is now concentrated on the Fraser and Skeena Rivers.

Aquaculture in British Columbia is a **growing industry**. In 1989 there were 592 operations running 226 salmon farms, 173 trout farms, 437 oyster farms and 50 hatcheries. Altogether they produced 12,000 t with a value of $79 million.

There are about **223 fish processing companies** in British Columbia.

AGRICULTURE

Farming

The **first farming to be recorded** west of the Rocky Mountains began in 1811 in the Fort St. James area. In that year Daniel (or David) William Harmon grew an excellent crop of vegetables and barley.

In 1892 a Japanese businessman in Vancouver initiated **the first shipment of wheat** to Japan, worth $3,100.

The **first farm in the northern Okanagan** was established by Alexander Leslie Fortune, one of the "Overlanders" Fraser River group.

Canada's **most advanced grain terminal** is Prince Rupert Grain. "A joint effort of six of Canada's largest grain companies and farmer-owned co-ops," it is a computer-controlled terminal which now ships about 30% of west coast grain exports.

By weight, grain is the **largest export item** leaving B.C. ports.

A man named Scott, a miner turned rancher, was the **first person to grow tobacco** west of the Rockies — in the Lillooet area. No known date.

Livestock

Canada's **oldest ranch** is The Alkali Lake Ranch in B.C.'s interior. It had its beginning when the land was preempted on March 19, 1863 and the following year five hundred head of cattle (Texas longhorns) were driven up from "Oregon Territory." Although many farms in Canada had beef cattle, this apparently was the first, true, open-range cattle ranch.

The Gang Ranch may be the largest ranch in Canada but it definitely is not the largest ranch in the world. "You could drop 20 Gang Ranches into one of the northern Australian ranches and not be able to find them," according to an article in the Vancouver Sun, Oct. 25, 1986.

Indians fishing at the head of Moricetown Canyon between Smithers and New Hazelton.

The first cattle and horse ranching in the Okanagan probably was started inadvertently by John Haynes, the first law enforcement officer appointed to the area, or by his deputy W.H. Lowe, in the early 1870s. Some of the miners and settlers were disillusioned and discouraged, after struggling over the Dewdney Trail, and either quit at Osoyoos and sold their livestock to Haynes or Lowe or simply abandoned what was left and headed back or south.

British Columbia's livestock population consists of approx. 634,000 cattle, 243,000 pigs and 33,000 sheep.

Orchards

In 1874, B.C.'s **first large commercial apple orchard** was planted in the Okanagan Valley. The first carload of apples was not shipped until 1898.

The **first orchard** in the Creston area was started by John C. Rykert in 1884.

On February 1, 1889 at a small meeting in Vancouver, 93 fruit growers got together and formed the **British Columbia Fruit Growers Association** (BCFGA). During the next forty years they encountered many marketing problems and in 1939 the growers formed B.C. Tree Fruits Ltd. to market all their products under one brand name in a pooling system that was developed to ensure all the growers, large and small, would get their fair share of the market value.

In December, 1892, **the first shipload** of Japanese Mandarin Oranges landed in Vancouver. This was a test shipment to determine whether or not these oranges would be popular enough to be received annually in time for the festive season.

The Sun Rype plant in Kelowna, in 1988, is one of the **most up to date and efficient plants** of its kind in North America. It processes over 100 million pounds of B.C. fruit per year. It makes enough pie fillings to bake 1.5 million pies per year and also has the capacity to produce 40,000 cases of fruit juices per day.

Today B.C. Tree Fruits Ltd. is **the largest fruit marketing agency in North America**. The company exports about 35% of the local annual apple crop, of which 50% goes offshore and 50% to the U.S.

Kiwi fruit growing is an up and coming industry in the orchards of B.C.

The Okanagan Valley contains **90% of Canada's orchards**, with McIntosh and Delicious apples the main product.

Land

Only **four percent of British Columbia's total land area** is considered suitable for agriculture.

B.C. has an estimated 7.4 million ha (18.2 million acres) of open and forested grazing land.

There are about **19,000 farms in British Columbia**. Farm cash receipts in 1989 were about $1.2 billion.

British Columbia farms produce more than **80 different food items** and this equals almost 60% of its own food requirements.

Close to **60% of B.C.'s greenhouses** are in Surrey.

Pokey and Donna at Canim Lake. Pokey is the community mascot and wanders around whereever he pleases — at 800 lbs, who is going to stop him?

Odds & Ends

Food and beverage production in B.C. in 1989 had a value of about $3.4 billion.

B.C. imports over half of its agricultural needs.

Over **90% of Canada's cranberries** are grown in British Columbia.

British Columbia accounts for 21% of Canada's turkey production and 10% of the chicken production.

On February 1, 1903, Mrs. William McDermott, of Burnaby, had a black Minorca hen which laid **an egg measuring 19 cm by 16.5 cm** (7 1/2 by 6 1/2 in.) and weighing 85 g (3 oz.).

Gardens

According to Guinness a "sunflower" measuring 81.9 cm (32 1/4 in.) in diameter was grown by Mrs. Emily Martin of Maple Ridge, B.C., in September of 1983.

The **largest Begonia plant** ever grown was over 1.1 m (3 ft. 8 in.) tall. It was grown in Richmond by Ellen Cassidy in 1979 (1981 Guinness Book of World Records).

The **largest rhododendron bush** in B.C. is in Fort Langley.

Victoria's **annual flower count** takes place in February. The highest count to date occurred in February of 1987: 203,241,053 blossoms. Last year's count (1991) was 154,580,731.

MISCELLANEOUS

Private Business

On July 29, 1858, Wellington Delaney Moses, a Californian, opened **the first barber shop** in B.C. at Fort Victoria. It even had a bath.

The **first Chinese businessman** to set up shop in B.C. was Kwong Lee in Victoria in 1858. A Hong Kong importer-retailer, his business was in general merchandise (including opium, which was legal at the time). He opened branch offices in New Westminster in 1860, in Quesnel in 1864, in Barkerville in 1866, and in Quesnel Forks, Yale and Lillooet in 1868. This solidly established him as operating the first "chain store" in B.C. In 1860 Kwong Lee brought his wife over from China and she thus became the first Chinese woman in B.C.

The **second bank** to open in B.C. was the Bank of British Columbia, opened in New Westminster in 1862. It closed within two months due to a lack of coins. Other branches stayed open for several years in Quesnel, Barkerville, Richfield and Victoria.

The **oldest, continuously licensed, hotel** in B.C. is the Six Mile House at Millstream (Victoria). It has been licensed since 1855.

The Lorne Hotel in Comox, B.C., also claims to be the **"Oldest Licensed Hotel in B.C."** It was built in 1867.

The **first hot food delivery service** in B.C. was proclaimed at Barkerville, in June, 1865 by this ad in the Sentinel: "The Original Pieman — Hot pies of the best description supplied to parties at their own residence at twenty-five cents each. Joseph Revis."

The **first credit union** in B.C. opened in 1936 in South Burnaby. Various accounts give their assets at the time as being from $10.25 to $75.00. Another story (from *Bygones of Burnaby*) says that as they could not afford to pay for their charter at that time, the Powell River Credit Union was first to receive theirs.

Trade

In 1873 **Canadian trade with Japan started** with small amounts of green tea being the main commodity.

Shipments by the manufacturing industry in British Columbia in 1989 had a total value of $25,877,000,000.

GARDENS

Unfortunately, space does not permit me to describe all the fantastic gardens in British Columbia. This is a list of some of the better known ones:

- Butchart Gardens,
    Vancouver Island
- Cominco Gardens,
    Kimberley
- Dr. Sun Yat-Sen Chinese Garden,
    Vancouver
- Fantasy Garden World,
    Richmond
- Minter Gardens,
    Rosedale
- Park & Tilford Gardens,
    North Vancouver
- U.B.C. Botanical Gardens,
    Vancouver
- VanDusen Botanical Gardens,
    Vancouver

The latest figures (Fall 1991) show B.C. has **total exports** of about $17 billion, the major items being softwood lumber, wood pulp, paper and paperboard, coal and copper.

The **value of retail trade** in British Columbia in 1989 was $20.5 billion. This was a 10.2% increase over the previous year.

Retail sales in B.C. shopping centres increased during 1990 by 8.4% over 1989 figures. This was the best in Canada which overall carried an average 4.2% increase.

Unions

The **Western Federation of Miners** (WFM) was officially formed in Butte, Montana, in 1893. The first Canadian local was established in 1895 in Rossland, B.C. and they were instrumental in convincing the provincial government to bring in North America's first "eight-hour day" legislation.

Over 37% of all British Columbia's workers are **unionized**. (The largest unions in B.C. are the B.C. Government Employees Union, the Canadian Union of Public Employees, the International Woodworkers of America and the B.C. Teachers' Federation.

The largest union in B.C. is the British Columbia Government Employees Union (B.C.G.E.U.) with membership of over 50,000.

This is a monument to John Jaques Caux, better known as "Cataline." He was the best packer in B.C. and quite possibly North America and played a major role in opening up the Interior. In his lifetime it became accepted that "Cataline" would never fail to fulfill a freight contract.

Industry

In 1950 the **first regional shopping centre** in Western Canada was established at Park Royal in West Vancouver. The major firm in the centre is Woodward's.

Today the Guildford Town Centre Mall is **the largest mall** in British Columbia.

The **first McDonald's Restaurant** in Canada opened in Richmond in 1967.

There are over 1.4 million employed workers in British Columbia of which about 56% are male and 44% female.

Approximately 74% of British Columbia's workers are in the "provision of services" sector while 26% are in the "goods-producing" sector.

The Provincial Public Service of B.C. employs over 30,000 people. Federally, employees in B.C. number over 26,000 and Municipal employees total about 24,000.

B.C.'s wineries have grown into a large industry, especially in the Okanagan area. During October there are a great number of wine festivals, parties and tasting events, beginning with a wine auction. Most of the wineries offer free tastings and tours. For more information call 1-800-663-5052.

The Hiram Walker Distillery at Winfield B.C. is the **second largest distillery** in Canada — second only to its parent company in Windsor, Ontario.

Odds & Ends

The **first sale of town lots** in B.C. was in the fall of 1858. This was at a public auction conducted by the government. The auction was in Victoria and the lots were at Fort Langley. The government realized $66,000.00 from this sale.

Moodyville (North Vancouver) was the only community north of San Francisco with **electric lights** in 1890.

The **first hydro-electric plant** in B.C. was established at Bonnington Falls on the Kootenay River near Nelson in 1897.

The first houses in Canada to be built to **metric standards** were in North Burnaby, B.C. in 1977.

On October 13, 1977, Premier Bill Bennett officially opened the Mica Dam, **the largest earth-fill dam** in the world, outside the C.I.S. Located 144 km (89.5 mi.) north of Revelstoke, on Highway 23, it is 243.8 m (800 ft.) high and will eventually have a capacity of 2604 MW. McNaughton Lake, created by the dam, stretches 216 km (134.2 mi.)

through previously forested areas. Before this lake (reservoir) was filled, enough timber to build 100,000 homes was salvaged.

The 1986 Guinness Book of World Records says the **brightest lights in the world** are made in B.C. The 300,000 W light bulb is produced by Vorteck Industries and was developed after research at the University of British Columbia came up with a new cooling method that broke the 20,000 W barrier.

Building permits issued in British Columbia during 1989 had a value of $5,221,000,000.00.

LOTTERIES

In 1974 the four western provinces formed a partnership to conduct lotteries, within their jurisdictions, called the Western Canada Lottery Federation (WCLF). In 1985 British Columbia withdrew from the WCLF and formed their own organization called the **British Columbia Lottery Corporation**.

Today the BCLC is the **second largest crown corporation** in B.C. (based on profit generated for the government). It also has the third highest average weekly sales per capita in North America. The BCLC directly employs 354 people, excluding the 2,100 retailers around the province. In British Columbia the Lottery Grants Branch, under the direction of the Provincial Secretary, administers the grant programs financed by the British Columbia Lottery Fund.

The **top ten lottery prizes** in B.C. have ranged from $3,907,297 to $7,789,787.60. (The top ten prizes in Canada have ranged from $10,000,000 to $13,964,107.40 (Figures to November 18, 1991).

ELECTRICAL POWER

In 1989 British Columbia generating stations produced **57,655 gigawatt hours of thermal-electric power**. (A gigawatt hour is a measurement representing the energy required to deliver one watt of electricity for one billion hours, or enough energy to serve one hundred typical households for one year.)

In addition to **thousands of kilometres of power lines** operating at distribution voltage, B.C. Hydro has the following primary power transmission lines in service: 5,263 km of 500 Kilovolt lines; 3,968 km of 360, 287 and 230 kilovolt lines; 4,159 km of 138 kilovolt lines; 3,807 km of 60 kilovolt lines. B.C. connects with Alberta and Washington State by 500 kilovolt transmission lines (1986 figures).

The Revelstoke Dam and Generating Station is one of North America's **largest and most modern hydroelectric developments**. It is owned and operated by B.C. Hydro and is located 4 km north of Revelstoke, B.C.

The **largest private hydroelectric reservoir** in B.C. is Ootsa Lake, which is controlled at Skins Dam spillway. This is located near François Lake in B.C.'s Lakes District.

THE ODDS

What are the odds on winning the major prize in B.C. lotteries?

6/49	1 in 13,983,816
Extra	1 in 3,764,376
Lotto B.C.	1 in 3,838,380
Keno	1 in 1,159,587
Daily	1 in 333,333
Provincial	1 in 1,000,000

TOURISM

B.C.'s **second largest industry** is Tourism. Total revenues from this source in 1988 reached $3.5 billion. 12.7 million people travelled in B.C. for one or more nights, another six million were excursionists (travelling more than 80 km from home but not overnight). British Columbians themselves accounted for 57% of the tourist population and they spent 43.5% of the total revenues.

There are over **140 Travel Info Centres** in British Columbia. They will give you helpful information including literature and trip planning whether it be for a day or the whole season.

Almost **$4 billion was spent** in British Columbia by tourists in 1989.

Cruise ships stopping at the Port of Vancouver, on their way to Alaska, carried 423,928 passengers in 1990. This figure was up 9.2% over the previous year and was the ninth consecutive year of passenger increase.

"**Super Show B.C.**" is a travelling caravan of two custom built semi-trailer show trucks, a 40 foot motorhome and several support vehicles. These vehicles have artwork on their sides which was designed and air brushed by graphic artists to depict B.C.'s many attractions. The show was created by Marty Vanderhoek. It is on a two-year tour of most major centres in North America to promote British Columbia.

CHAPTER 8

WEATHER

British Columbia holds more **weather related records** than any other province in Canada.

B.C., especially its coastal areas, is **well known for its rain**, and yet, there are some places in B.C. that are the driest in Canada.

At Cape St. James, on the Queen Charlotte Islands, there is a **very important Pacific Coast weather station** and lighthouse. There are few flat spots so the three buildings here, are on different levels, inter-connected by a miniature railway running up the steep incline. The wind speed here has been recorded at over 100 km/h (62 mph) almost 30% of the time, with gusts exceeding hurricane force. During a storm on October 26, 1985 one gust was recorded at 190 km/h (118 mph).

The **only desert in Canada** is in the south Okanagan at Osoyoos. Here they have an average rainfall of only 25.4 cm (10 in.). Most of this desert has been transformed into orchards with the aid of irrigation.

Victoria and the Gulf Islands can be considered to have a **Mediterranean climate**.

July 11 is outstanding because "**more notable weather events** occurred on this day than any other."

October 2 — The Canadian Weather Trivia Calendar records the following for this day: "Some days are more eventful than others, but **October 2** is noteworthy because nothing happened on this day. To the best of our knowledge, this date is devoid of major storms, unseasonal heat or cold waves, or untimely frosts and snows. Today's forecast is for no surprises. Enjoy it!"

Climate Severity Index (CSI) is a scale, from 1 to 100, which was devised by Environment Canada to rate the average climate of any given area, with all conditions being taken into account. The lower the number, the better the climate. Of all the major Canadian cities, Victoria, B.C., was best at 13 and St. John's, NFLD. worst at 56. Vancouver came in second with a score of 18.

Have you ever noticed a little structure, like the one shown in the photograph, along any highway or road? This one is at Fish Lake on Hwy. 31A in the West Kootenay. This is an unmanned weather station from which readings are taken on a regular schedule. Most of these stations are maintained by the Dept. of Highways. What do meteorologists learn from these stations? Lots — the amount of precipitation (rain in millimetres and snow in centimetres); the rate of precipitation per hour, and the precipitation to date by the month; wind direction; wind velocity; the high and low temperature of the past 24 hours; relative humidity; amount of snow on the ground, how much snow in a particular storm, and in the past 24 hours.

HEAT & SUN

The **highest temperature ever recorded** in B.C. was 44.4°C (112°F) on July 16 and 17, 1941. It occurred in three places at the same time: Chinook Cove, Lillooet and Lytton. The highest in Canada is 45°C (113°F), and the world high recorded in Mexico was 58°C (136.4°F). Al'azizyah, Libya also recorded a temperature of 58°C on September 13, 1922.

Victoria recorded its **record high temperature** of 36.1°C (96.98°F) on July 16, 1941.

Vancouver's **highest temperature** was 33.3°C (91.9°F) on Aug. 18, 1908.

Kamloops, B.C. **holds the record** for having the most days per year with temperatures of at least 35°C (95°F). They average 8 days per year, but in 1958 they had 24 days.

Cranbrook has the **highest average annual bright sunshine** in B.C.: 2,244 hours.

Stewart has the **least Average Annual Bright Sunshine** in B.C.: 949 hours.

The **average warmest annual temperature** in Canada occurs at Sumas Canal: 10.7°C.

The Okanagan has **more hours of sunshine** per year than Florida.

RAIN

B.C. has also been called the **rain capital of Canada**.

Total rainfall in British Columbia averages approximately 25.5 billion litres (5.6 billion) gallons per day, an amount equivalent to total fresh water consumption in the United States.

Well known for its rain, **Vancouver is actually drier** than Edmonton, Regina, Winnipeg, Toronto, Ottawa, Montréal and Halifax for the months of June, July and August. Vancouver is also drier during the summer than most American cities east of the Rocky Mountains.

The **worst avalanche disaster** in B.C.'s history was the mudslide at Britannia Beach in 1915 which left 57 persons dead. It was caused by heavy rains.

The towns of Squamish and Pemberton were **devastated by flooding** at the end of October in 1981. Records from Seymour Falls show that Oct. 30th had 206 mm (8 in.) of rain and Oct. 31st a further 200 mm (7.8 in.).

On Sept. 16, 1988, **a spectacular thunderstorm** and torrential rains lashed the lower mainland of B.C., pitching 25,000 homes into darkness, causing floods, and snarling traffic. Hail added to traffic problems on the Lions Gate Bridge in Vancouver. Strong thunderclaps set off burglar alarms, and telephone equipment failures were common.

Ashcroft has the **least amount of average annual precipitation** of any place in B.C.: 205.6 mm (8.1 in.).

The **greatest amount of precipitation** in one year in Canada was 8,122.4 mm (320 in.) at Henderson Lake, B.C. The greatest average annual precipitation, 6,655 mm (262 in.), also occurs here. The world's record is 26,461 mm (1042 in.) at Cherrapunji, India.

The Canadian record of **greatest rainfall in one day** is 489.2 mm (19 in.) at Ucluelet Brynnor Mines, Vancouver Island, on Oct. 6, 1967. The world record one day rainfall is 1,870 mm (73.6 in.) on Mar. 15, 1952 at La Reunion Island in the Indian Ocean.

The **greatest monthly rainfall** ever recorded in Canada was 2,235.5 mm (88 in.) at Swanson Bay, B.C. in November 1917. Coming in second is Henderson Lake, B.C. with 2,018.5 mm (80 in.) in December, 1923.

The **heaviest rainfall** in a 24-hour period recorded at the Vancouver International Airport was 92.7 mm (3.65 in.), on December 25, 1972.

A **Canadian rainfall record** for six hours was set on Jan. 26, 1984 at McInnes Island, B.C. It was 265 mm (10 in.).

On Oct. 14, 1934 at Red Creek, B.C., it **rained tiny beetles** intermittently for three hours.

SNOW & COLD

The **greatest average annual snowfall** in Canada is 1,433 cm (564 in.) and occurs at Glacier National Park, Mt. Fidelity, B.C.

The **greatest snowfall in one season**, in Canada, was 2,446.5 cm (963 in.) during the winter of 1971/1972 at Revelstoke/Mount Copeland, B.C.

Revelstoke has the **heaviest snowfall** of any city on the Trans Canada Highway.

Rogers Pass, at 1,330 m (4,364 ft.) above sea level has an average annual snowfall of 870 cm (342 in.), **one of the heaviest in the world.**

The **greatest snowfall in one month**, in Canada, was 525.9 cm (207 in.) at Haines Apps. No. 2 B.C. in December 1959.

The **greatest one day snowfall** in Canada was 118.1 cm (47 in.) at Lakelse, B.C. on Jan. 17, 1974.

Carnation Creek, B.C., has the **least Average Annual Snowfall** of any place in Canada: 20.4 cm (8 in.).

The **record snowfall for a 24-hour period** in Victoria is 61 cm (24 in.) set on January 7, 1880.

Vancouver's greatest snowfall for a one-month period was 140 cm (55 in.), which occurred in January, 1913. Vancouver has, on average, one white Christmas every ten years.

The **lowest temperature** ever recorded in B.C. was -58.8°C (-74°F) on January 31, 1947 at Smith River. Only two other spots in Canada have been colder: Fort Vermillion, Alberta, -61.1°C (-78°F) on January 11, 1911 and Snag, Yukon, -62.7°C (-81°F) on February 3, 1947. The world low was recorded at Vostok, Antarctica on August 24, 1960: -89.9°C (-129.9°F).

An average of **108 Canadians die each year** from exposure to extreme cold, far more than the number killed by lightning, tornadoes, winds, floods and heat waves.

The coldest average annual **temperature** in British Columbia is -3.2°C (26.2°F) at Cassiar.

A **hailstorm** in the Okanagan Valley near Penticton, B.C., on July 29, 1946, did $2 million damage to the apple and pear crops in 15 minutes. Some hailstones measured over 5 cm (2 in.) in diameter.

CHAPTER 9

MILITARY

The Royal Westminster Regiment (Motor), closely connected with the Royal Engineers, is the **oldest military unit** in British Columbia. Queen Victoria dispatched this group in 1859 to establish law and order and help in opening up this westernmost outpost of the British Empire.

The British Columbia Regiment (Royal Canadian Armoured Corps), first created October 12, 1883, claims to be **the oldest militia unit** in B.C.

The **Vernon Military Camp** was established in 1908 and was, for many years, the largest camp in B.C., training soldiers for two world wars.

On August 5, 1914 British Columbia became the only province in Canada to ever **purchase their own warships**. The British Empire went to war on August 4, 1914 and, at the time, there seemed to be an urgent need to protect the west coast of Canada. Two submarines built for Chile were in Seattle, Wash. Chile couldn't meet the payment requirements and Premier Richard McBride of B.C. took it upon himself to purchase these two subs for the price of $1,150,000. Three days later Ottawa "assumed responsibility for the purchase" and these boats thus became Canada's first submarines. Considered to be of the "C" class, they were designated CC1 and CC2. The two subs remained in service on the Pacific coast (based at Esquimalt) for almost three years. They left Esquimalt on June 21, 1917 for Halifax. On August 12, 1917 they became the first warships flying the White Ensign to pass through the Panama Canal.

The Town of Walachin, B.C. (now a ghost town) became the **most patriotic community** in Canada when 40 of its 41 bachelors signed up for service at the start of the First World War. It was the fastest, and proportionally largest, mass enlistment for any town in Canada.

In British Columbia **10% of the province's population enlisted** and served in the military during the First World War. About 43,000 enlisted out of which almost 20,000 were killed or wounded.

The **Air Cadet movement** in Canada began in 1940 at Vancouver. The Air Cadet League of Canada was formed in 1941.

Heather Erxleber, a resident of B.C., became the **first female combat soldier** in Canada, when she graduated at Canadian Forces Base Wainwright, Alberta, on Jan. 19, 1989. She was one of sixteen women who began the sixteen week training course (with the men) and was the only woman to complete it. "It is a very physically demanding course," said the 22-year-old native of Vancouver, B.C.

VICTORIA CROSS

Since its inception in 1854, ninety-three Canadians have received the Victoria Cross, once the highest military distinction of the British Commonwealth. Of these, fifty-two were born in Canada. Five were from British Columbia. Their names, place of birth and date of award was as follows:

Charles Cecil Merritt	Vancouver	Aug. 19, 1942
Charles Ferguson Hoey	Duncan	Feb. 16, 1944
John Keefer Mahony	New Westminster	May 24, 1944
Ernest Alvia Smith	New Westminster	Oct. 21, 1944
Robert Hampton Gray	Trail	Aug. 9, 1945

It is extremely rare to find two V.C.'s from the same city, in this case New Westminster, but what is even more unusual is the fact that they lived within two blocks of each other.

Since the first edition of this book, John Keefer Mahony VC, CD, passed away in St. Mary's Hospital Dec. 15, 1990.

CHAPTER 10

SPORTS

SKIING

The **first ski club** in Canada was formed in Revelstoke, B.C., during the winter of 1891.

The **first Canadian Downhill Ski Championships** were held at Rossland, B.C. in 1897.

The **first Dominion Cup Ski Championships** were held at Rossland, B.C. in 1900.

Red Mountain Ski Hill at Rossland, B.C. was one of the **first ski resorts** to be developed in North America. It also had the first chair lift in Western Canada.

The **first Canadian to win a gold medal** at the Olympics was Nancy Greene, of Rossland, in 1968. She was named as Canada's outstanding female athlete of 1967 and 1968.

Canada's **first World Cup Ski event**, the Du Maurier International, was held at Rossland, B.C. March 28-31, 1968. It was organized by the Canadian Amateur Ski Association.

Whistler Resort "skististics" for Winter 1991/1992 shows their average annual snowfall on the summit is over 11 m (36 ft.). Blackcomb Mountain has thirteen lifts with a combined capacity of 23,850 skiers per hour, and Whistler Mountain has twelve lifts with a capacity of 22,295 skiers per hour. Each mountain has over a hundred marked runs and both are rated 25% expert, 55% intermediate, and 20% beginner. Whistler Resort has a permanent population of about 3,500.

In British Columbia there are about 608,000 downhill skiers and 422,000 cross-country skiers.

On February 26, 1989, Rob Boyd became the **first Canadian to win** Canada's premier skiing event, the "Molson World Downhill," at Whistler, B.C.

The Murray Ridge Ski Hill at Fort St. James, B.C. claims to have the **longest T-Bar lift** in North America. Murray Ridge has a Dopplemayr lift with a length of 1,981.2 m (6,500 ft.).

The **longest double chair lift** in North America is on Todd Mountain, (Kamloops, B.C.). It is 3.3 km (2 mi.) in length and has a vertical climb of 942 m (3,100 ft.).

Dave Phillips and Garry O'Neil set a **world record for non-stop skiing**. Their feat, lasting 83 hours 17 minutes, took place on Grouse Mountain and ended February 23, 1986.

Silver Star Mountain Ski Resort in Vernon is one of the many great ski facilities in the province. This one has a very distinct western flavour.

One of the many interesting "characters" you'll find at Silver Star.

HOCKEY

The **first professional hockey team** west of Winnipeg was at Grand Forks, B.C., in 1906.

The **first covered natural ice rink** in B.C. was built at Grand Forks in the fall of 1906.

The **first hockey trophy** in B.C. was the Boundary Hockey Championship Cup and it was first won by Grand Forks in the 1908-09 season.

The Stanley Cup is the "**oldest trophy** competed for by professional athletes in North America." In the 1914-15 hockey season it was won by the Vancouver Millionaires, of the Pacific Coast Hockey League, by defeating the Ottawa Senators three games straight in a best-of-five series. In the 1924-25 season the Victoria Cougars won it by defeating the Montreal Maroons in four games, also in a best-of-five series.

The **first hockey game** ever played on artificial ice was at Victoria on January 3, 1912. The New Westminster Royals beat the Victoria Aristocrats by an 8-3 score.

On October 9, 1970, the Vancouver Canucks hockey team played their **first NHL game** and lost 3-1 to the L.A. Kings.

FOOTBALL

The B.C. Lions Football Club played their **first game** on August 28, 954 against the Winnipeg Blue Bombers at Empire Stadium. Winnipeg won by a score of 8 to 6.

The **B.C. Lions won the Grey Cup** on November 28, 1964. The game was played in Toronto against the Hamilton Tiger Cats. The final score was B.C. 34, Hamilton 24.

The **first Grey Cup game played on artificial turf** was in Vancouver in 1971 and the first Grey Cup game played indoors was also in Vancouver in 1983.

BASEBALL

The first organized baseball in B.C. was played in Barkerville in 1864. One of these first organizers, and a player himself, was Thomas H. Pattullo, the uncle of Thomas Duff Pattullo, Premier of B.C. from 1933-41.

On Oct. 11, 1957, the Vancouver Mounties baseball team was **fined $150** for playing baseball on a Sunday.

James Donaldson Park, in Grand Forks, B.C., claims to be "**Home of Western Canada's Largest Invitational Baseball Tournament.**"

GAMES

The **1989 B.C. Winter Games** were held in Nelson, B.C. Over 2,200 athletes and officials from all over the province participated in 27 different sporting events.

The **1994 Commonwealth Games**, with athletes expected from over 60 countries, will be held at Victoria, B.C.

Ironman Canada — This grueling international event is an annual affair in Penticton. It began in 1983 and it now attracts over 800 participants from around the world. It consists of a 4 km (2 1/2 mi.) swim followed by 180.3 km (112 mi.) of cycling and ending with a 42.2 km (26.2 mi.) marathon run.

The World's Largest Cross Country Skis are found in 100 Mile House. They are 12m (39.4 ft) in length. They were made in recognition of the South Cariboo's stature as a cross-country skiing centre of Western Canada.

TITLES & RECORDS

In 1928, Percy Williams of Vancouver **set a world record** in the 100 m run in the Amsterdam Olympics.

In 1953, Douglas Hepburn of Vancouver, B.C., despite a bad leg and a sprained ankle, won the **World Weightlifting Championship** held in Stockholm.

"The Miracle Mile" was accomplished on Aug. 7, 1954 when two men broke the four-minute barrier in the same race. It happened during the British Empire Games held at Empire Stadium in Vancouver. Roger Bannister won with a time of 3.58:8 minutes; John Landy who in second with a time of 3.59:6 minutes. The very first issue of Sports Illustrated featured the story of the "Miracle Mile" in Vancouver.

Cairn in Victoria: "This Cairn Commemorates The Feat of Miss Marilyn Bell who landed in the Bay 23rd August, 1956 to become the first woman and first Canadian to **swim Juan de Fuca Strait** from Port Angeles, U.S.A. to Victoria, Canada."

Jube Wickheim, of Shawnigan Lake, B.C., won **ten World Championships** in Birling (log-rolling) from 1956 to 1969.

Elaine Tanner of Vancouver, carried the nickname **"Mighty Mouse"** because of her performance in international swimming competitions. She was Canada's Outstanding Athlete in 1966 at age 15 and was awarded the Order of Canada in 1969.

Karen Magnussen of North Vancouver, B.C., won the **Women's World Figure Skating title** at Bratislava, Czechoslovakia in 1973. She had previously been taken out of the world championship competitions at Colorado Springs in 1969 because of a fractured bone but ultimately she went on to win the Canadian championship three years in a row, and then the world title. She then turned professional and joined the "Ice Capades."

On July 18, 1977, Willie Shoemaker, **the world's leading jockey**, attracted over 11,500 fans to the races in Vancouver, who for the first time in the track's history, wagered more than $1 million.

The plaque on this statue reads:
"THE WILL TO DO,
THE SOUL TO DARE"

HARRY WINSTON JEROME
Born September 30, 1940
Died December 7, 1982

WORLD RECORDS
1960 100 yards 9.3 seconds
1960 100 metres 10.0 seconds
1962 100 yards 9.2 seconds
1962 4x110 yards relay 40.0 seconds
1964 60 yards 6.0 seconds
1966 100 yards 9.1 seconds

1971 Order of Canada

On May 17, 1978, Victoria gymnast Philip Delasalle, became the **first Canadian** ever in international competition, to score a perfect 10 out of 10.

According to Guinness the **fastest time for a 1.6 km (1 mi.) wheelbarrow race** was 4 minutes, 52.04 seconds. This was accomplished at the Ladner Centennial Sports Festival at Delta, B.C. on July 6, 1980. John Cortes and Brian Rhodes of Richmond, B.C., were the two winning participants.

Daniel Westley, a Canada Post employee in the Pacific Division, is one of the **top wheelchair athletes** in the world. He is the holder of several world records and medals and has, in fact, been called "the fastest human on wheels." In 1981 he was named British Columbia's Disabled Athlete of the Year.

In July, 1982, Ed Johnson of Victoria, B.C., made **the fastest climb** up a 30.5 m (100 ft.) fir spar pole and return to the ground for a record of 27.16 seconds, at the Lumberjack World Championships in Hayward, Wis.

Linda Moore's North Vancouver Rec. Centre rink won the **Women's World Curling Championship** in Sweden March 23, 1985 by defeating Scotland in the final game. It was the first time a rink from B.C. had won and also the first time the same country had won two years in a row.

In the first year of the **World Junior Ladies Curling Championships** (1988), B.C.'s Julie Sutton rink emerged the winner.

ODDS & ENDS

The **first nine-hole golf course** in B.C. was established at Jericho by the Vancouver Golf Club in 1892.

The **northernmost golf course** in B.C. is at Fort Nelson.

The **first race track** (for horse racing) in British Columbia was at Race Track Creek in the Cariboo. The track itself was eight furlongs in length and races were held here for several years in the 1860s and 1870s. A two-storey casino and several smaller establishments were built here. Race Track Creek is between the heads of Williams Cr. and Antler Cr.

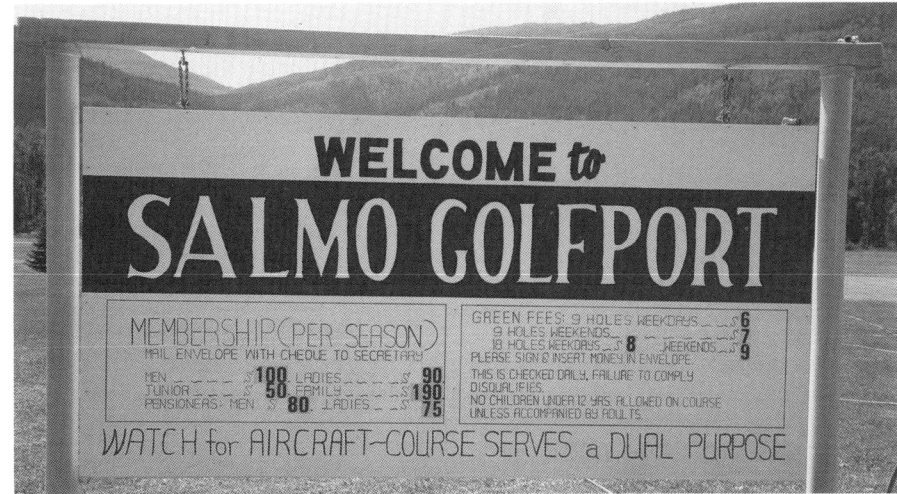

Canada's first combination airport and golf course is the Salmo Golf Port. This is a unique 9-hole golf course, laid out along the perimeter of an airport, with the ninth hole crossing the grassy runway. Aircraft are required to "buzz" the area before landing.

The tennis centre at the UBC offers the **largest number of tennis programs** in Western Canada.

Plaque on wall in bar of Smithers Hotel, Smithers, B.C.: "This picture is to commemorate the **international darts match** played over the telephone between Smithers Hotel, B.C. and the Royal Oak Copmanthorpe, York, England, on February 11th, 1984."

The **B.C. Sports Hall of Fame and Museum**, formerly in the B.C. Pavilion on the PNE grounds in Vancouver, officially opened their Phase One in B.C. Place Stadium, January, 1992. These new facilities were intended to be "a tribute to the province's athletes and builders as well as a high-tech, hands-on sports entertainment centre." With the completion of its third phase in 1993, it is expected the centre will become one of the top ten tourist attractions in the province.

B.C. PLACE STADIUM

B.C. Place Stadium was the first multi-use amphitheatre, or domed stadium in Canada. Here are some statistics:

Size of stadium: 189.9m (623ft.) wide,
231.6m (760ft.) long,
762m (2500ft.) in circumference,
60.9m (200ft.) high.

Covers ten acres with three acres of plazas. The roof is teflon-coated fibreglass with a total weight of 280 tons (including cables, lights, sound equipment, etc.) all of which is held up by 16 fans of 100 hp each. Construction took 1.5 million man hours on site. Over four million kilograms of steel were used along with 53,000 cubic meters of concrete.

- Construction Time: 28 months.
- Cost: $126 million
- Seats: 60,000
- Officially opened: June 19, 1983
- Food and Beverage outlets: 36
- Washrooms: 72
- Video Screen: 5.5m x 12.2m (18ft. x 40ft.), with 200 closed circuit TVs in public areas
- Exhibition Space: 13,935 m² (150,000 sq. ft.) at field level, 7,432 m² (80,000 sq. ft.) on the second level.
- Staff: 48 full time employees, up to 1,000 part-time workers.

In its first two and a half months over a million people came to see a wide variety of events at B.C. Place Stadium

CHAPTER 11

LAW & ORDER

HISTORY

The **first hostage-taking incident** in B.C. occurred on Mar. 22, 1803 when Natives attacked the schooner Boston, massacring 25 of the 27 crewmen and holding the other two as slaves.

On November 19, 1858, Matthew Baillie Begbie was appointed to the post of Chief Justice of British Columbia. He was known as **"The Hanging Judge"** in B.C.'s gold rush days, and he maintained law and order throughout the land for many years, but in fact, only sent two men to the scaffold.

In 1859, a group of American miners at Lytton, riled up at finding a loaf of bread had been stolen from their camp, discovered it had been taken by an elderly Native, and hanged him. This is the **first known incident of vigilantes** taking "justice" into their own hands in B.C.

During September of 1866 James Barry, a gambler, became the chief suspect in the murder of Charles Blessing on May 31. He left the Cariboo before he could be apprehended. Constable John H. Sullivan, under orders from the district head of police, Chief Constable W.F. Fitzgerald, in Richfield, set out in pursuit. Arriving at Soda Creek he discovered he had just missed his quarry who was on the stage for Yale. Sullivan approached the electric telegraph operator in Soda Creek who tapped out a message to the police at Yale. Barry was arrested as soon as he stepped off the stagecoach in Yale. This was the **first time the electric telegraph had been used** to catch a criminal in B.C.

Construction of the **Federal Penitentiary in New Westminster** began in 1874 and its first prisoners were received September 28, 1878. After more than a hundred years the prison was closed (February 15, 1980) in favor of "several

The Hangman's Tree in Lillooet. This old ponderosa pine was used as a gallows for the administration of justice more than 100 years ago. At the time the law was Sir Mathew Begbie, better known as "The Hanging Judge." Records that two thieves were hanged and buried here can be found but legend has it that eight lawbreakers in all swung from this tree. The bough which actually accomodated the noose has since rotted of, but the gnarled pine remains.

smaller institutions . . . better suited to modern needs." This site is now a residential area.

The **first mass execution** in B.C. was on January 31, 1881 when four members of the five-man McLean Gang were hanged for the murder of Constable John Ussher. He was murdered 25.7 km (16 mi.) south of Kamloops on December 7, 1879. Their execution took place in New Westminster. The four were Allan McLean, 25; Charles McLean, 17; Archie McLean, 15; and Alex Hare, 17. The fifth member of the gang, Hector McLean, was acquitted, as he was not with them at the time. He had made a plan to free the rest of the gang but it was found out in time to prevent its being carried out.

Vancouver's **first police constable**, Jonathan Miller, was appointed, on May 10, 1886, at the first city council meeting, which was being held in Mr. Miller's house.

The **first stagecoach hold-up** in Canada occurred on June 9, 1886 at Mile 82 on the Cariboo Road near Clinton. The driver, Ned Tate, was short $2,000 in gold bullion and he said the incident occurred on the same spot where he had reported an attempted holdup the previous summer. Mr. Tate quit his job shortly thereafter (June 30) and it was generally thought he robbed his own stage. This was never proven one way or the other.

On July 30, 1887, Colonel Samuel Steele arrived at Galbraith's Ferry, at the junction of Wild Horse Creek and the Kootenay River, with a force of 75 men and established the **first North West Mounted Police post** west of the Rocky Mountains. After settling some disputes between the miners and the Natives he had nothing to do and was forced to abandon his post, moving his detachment out August 7, 1888. The town was later renamed Fort Steele after the man who built it.

The **first train robbery** in Canadian history occurred on Sept. 10, 1904 when the Trans-continental Express No. 1 of the C.P.R. was held up at Silverdale, B.C. on its way into Vancouver. Silverdale is just outside of Mission in the Fraser Valley. The loot included $1,000 cash, $6,000 in gold dust and $50,000 in United States bonds. It was later generally accepted that this was the work of Bill Miner, but it was never proven one way or the other. Another hold-up of the Trans-continental at Monte Creek, east of Kamloops, on May 8, 1906 was quickly solved with the capture of Bill Miner and his two partners. They were convicted and sentenced to life imprisonment at the "Pen" in New Westminster. Bill Miner escaped from here August 8, 1907 and was never recaptured in Canada.

On November 1, 1909, the BX Stage (British Columbia Express) was robbed. Two weeks later a Mr. Clark was arrested as a suspect. His sister, Mrs. Reider, was also implicated. She was arrested in Ashcroft, November 18, 1909. After considerable discussion a constable opened the door to Mrs. Reider's cell and told her a train was now preparing to leave town. The **first alleged female stagecoach robber** was not long in finding her way to the railway station.

The Richfield Courthouse, built in 1882, is B.C.'s oldest surviving courthouse. By 1918, declining population in Richfield led to the buildings closure.

The bank robbery which, for many years, was **the largest in North America** occurred on the night of September 14, 1911. It was of the Bank of Montréal in New Westminster. The vaults were blown open and $258,000.00 was stolen. Very little of this money was ever recovered and no one was ever jailed.

During December of 1915 at Kamloops, Elizabeth "Betty" Coward, was the **first woman to be sentenced to death** in British Columbia. She had been convicted in October of the murder of her husband, Jim Coward, near Fort St. James on September 6. She was scheduled to be hanged December 23, but on the 21st was notified her sentence had been commuted to life imprisonment.

In 1917, Canada's **first female judge**, Helen Emma (Gregory) MacGill, was appointed to the bench of the Juvenile Court at Vancouver. Except for the years from 1929 to 1934, she held this position until her retirement in 1945.

On Oct. 20, 1920, British Columbia **voters rejected prohibition**.

On Oct. 11, 1923, women were allowed, for the first time, to sit as jurists. Francis Palmer, Helen Paton and Bertha Peterson were the **first three female jurors** in B.C.

The newly formed **"Association of Law Enforcement Officers of the Lower Mainland"** held their first meeting April 17, 1930. One of the main items of discussion was "the use of short wave radio equipment for rapid communication between district police departments."

In 1948, Andrew Joe became the **first Chinese-Canadian to graduate** from the University of B.C.'s law program and to be called to the bar. (Lawyer Harry Fan graduated a year earlier but had been unable to article.) It is only since 1947 that people of Chinese ancestry have been allowed to enter into such fields in Canada. Previously, government laws had prevented them from entering such professions as law, accounting and pharmacy.

The **first black lawyer** admitted to the B.C. bar was Ed Searles in October of 1957.

In 1974 at Terrace, B.C., Selwyn Romilly, at the age of 34, became the **first black judge** in British Columbia.

On September 22, 1976, Vancouver vice squad officers charged a man for propositioning a policewoman posing as a prostitute. It was the **first time a would-be**

customer was charged in Canada. As such, the man was given an absolute discharge, the judge commenting that the publicity was sufficient punishment this time, but would not be for future cases.

Doris Elva St. Germain, 28, was sworn in as the **first female Justice of the Peace** in Vancouver on November 1, 1976.

Judge Marjorie Cantryn of Burnaby became the **first Native** to be appointed to the court of Canadian Citizenship. Her appointment became effective March 1, 1977.

For the first time in B.C.'s history on July 1, 1977, the **R.C.M.P. used a helicopter** to assist ground units in traffic control. The experiment, which proved successful, was in the Duncan area and twenty charges were laid and nine other drivers given warnings.

The **largest drug bust** in B.C.'s history occurred May 22, 1979 when 30.5 t of marijuana was seized near Tofino, on Vancouver Island. The second largest bust was Aug. 17, 1988 when 20 t of marijuana from Thailand was seized in the Queen Charlotte Islands.

FACTS

British Columbia in 1990 had the **highest crime rate in Canada**: 14,957 offences per 100,000 population. Newfoundland was the lowest at 6,051 per 100,000 while the Canadian average was 9,903 per 100,000.

Vancouver had the highest crime rate in Canada in 1991 with a per capita rate of 21,176 per 100,000 residents. (Edmonton was second at 16,726 per 100,000 residents.)

The **rate of thefts from cars** in B.C. is 30.8 per 1,000 registered vehicles, the worst in Canada.

The British Columbia Provincial Police (BCPP) was formed in 1858 and served the law enforcement needs of the province for 92 outstanding years.

The Royal Canadian Mounted Police, on Aug. 15, 1950, became **the official law enforcement agency** of British Columbia. Assistant Commissioner A.T. Belcher was in charge.

R.C.M.P. Inspector Lew Dempsey, retired in June of 1985, was the **last member of the R.C.M.P.** to have served in the B.C. Provincial Police.

The R.C.M.P. Detachment headquartered in Cloverdale, Municipality of Surrey, is **the largest and busiest in Canada.**

In 1957 the federal government bought ten Chevrolet panel vans. They then sent one to each of the provincial capitals to be used for disaster services under the War Measures Act. As far as can be determined, at this point, the only one remaining is in the Edmonton Police Museum/Archives. If anyone out there has any information on any of these vehicles, or has had some connection with them, the Edmonton Police Museum/Archives would like to hear from you. Their mailing address is: 9620 - 103A Ave., Edmonton Alberta. T5H 0H7.

CHAPTER 12

IN & ON THE WATER

The following is quoted from Quick Facts About British Columbia: "An exceptionally rich resource is **B.C.'s abundance of waterways**—lakes, rivers and streams. Fresh water surfaces total two million hectares. These waterways support agriculture, hydro-electric power, fisheries and many recreational needs."

◆

B.C.'s **coastline is estimated at 27,000 km** and includes two massive island groups, Vancouver Island off the south coast and Queen Charlotte Islands to the north. Vancouver Island is the largest island in B.C., at 31,285 km², and the eleventh largest in Canada. Graham Island (largest island of the Queen Charlottes) is the second largest island in B.C. at 6,361 km², and the 22nd largest in Canada. The mainland coastline is about 7,022 km (4,363 mi.) long.

◆

B.C.'s **tallest underwater mountain** (or "seamount") is Bowie Seamount and it is approximately 3,300 m (10,826 ft.) high. It is located about 200 km (124 mi.) west of the Queen Charlotte Islands. The top of Bowie Seamount is about 300 m (984 ft.) below the surface of the Pacific Ocean.

◆

For coastal divers, mid-winter visibility in the "Emerald Sea" exceeds 20 m (66 ft.). With the abundance and diversity of marine life, **the area is a photographer's paradise.**

The **largest fjord** on B.C.'s coast is 193 km (120 mi.) long. It consists of Otter Passage and Gardner Canal.

◆

The **Native name** for the Queen Charlotte Islands is Haida Gwaii (pronounced Guwhy).

◆

Moresby Island, also in the Queen Charlottes, is **B.C.'s third largest island** at 2,787 km² (1,076 sq. mi.).

◆

Within the bounds of B.C. are **67 islands** of not less than 51.8 km² (20 sq. mi.) in size.

◆

The Japanese Current is responsible for the **warm temperature** of the waters off Canada's west coast, which are considerably warmer than waters at the same latitudes off Canada's east coast.

◆

According to Guinness, the **strongest currents in the world** are the Nakwakto Rapids, Slingsby Channel, B.C., where the flow rate may reach 16 knots (29.6 km/h or 18.4 mph).

◆

About 14 km (8.7 mi). south of Burns Lake is Tchesinkut Lake which, it is claimed, has **the purest water** in B.C.

The clear Thompson River (left) joining the muddy Fraser River at Lytton.

RIVERS

Ten of the twelve **longest rivers** in Canada are in Western Canada.

The **longest river in Canada** has its start in B.C. The MacKenzie River is 4,240.5 km (2,635 mi.) long from its source, the Finlay River in north central B.C, to its mouth, in the Arctic Ocean.

The Columbia River, originating from Columbia Lake in B.C., is the **fourth longest river** in North America. It has a length of over two thousand kilometres to where it empties into the Pacific Ocean near Astoria, Oregon.

The marshlands of the Columbia River Valley, in the East Kootenay area of B.C., has the **largest population of great blue herons** in Western Canada.

The B.C. **Championship Jet Boat Races** are held annually on the Columbia River between Trail and Castlegar.

The **Fraser River** is B.C.'s first and Canada's tenth longest river. The Fraser River also covers the largest drainage area in B.C. — 230,000 km² (89,000 sq. mi.).

Along the banks of the Fraser River can be found about 600 varieties of rocks and minerals including gold, jade, and many types of semi-precious stones such as agates, jasper, garnets and rubies.

One of many provincial Point-of-Interest signs located throughout the province. This one is found between Agassiz and Mission on the north side of the Fraser River.

An average 908 million litres (200 million gallons) of water, per minute, pass through the 34 m (110 ft.) wide **"Hell's Gate"** in the Fraser Canyon. In 1808 Simon Fraser said " . . . this is a place where no human beings should venture . . . it looks like the gates of hell."

The Kootenay River is Canada's **27th longest river** at 780 km (484.7 mi.).

The Skeena River is variously called the "River of the Clouds" and "River of the Mists."

The shortest river in British Columbia is also a major waterway. It is the Harrison River, which flows from Harrison Lake to the Fraser River — a distance of 19.3 km (12 mi.). It has a total average annual discharge of 14,200,000 cubic dekametres (one cubic dekametre equals 1,000 m³) and its average flow rate is 449 m³/s.

At approximately 350 km (217.5 mi.) north of the Yellowhead Highway, on the Cassiar Highway (No. 37), is **Eastman Creek**. It is named for a hunter of this area before the highway was built, George Eastman, of Eastman Kodak fame.

On the Cassiar Highway 494 km (306.9 mi.) north of the Yellowhead Highway, is **the divide between the watersheds** of the Pacific and Arctic Oceans.

LAKES

Atlin Lake in the northwest corner of the province is **the largest natural lake** in B.C. It covers an area of 562 km² (217 sq. miles) in B.C. and 72.5 km² (28 sq. miles) in the Yukon.

Babine Lake is B.C.'s **longest natural lake** at 177 km (110 mi.). It is also the largest natural lake entirely within B.C.: 497 km² (192 sq. mi.).

The **largest lake** in B.C. is man-made Lake Williston. It was formed behind the W.A.C. Bennett Dam and covers an area of 1761 km² (680 sq. mi.) at an elevation of 664.5 m (2180 ft.).

Kootenay Lake is B.C.'s **largest "year round open water lake."** It is approx. 144.8 km (90 mi.) long and covers an area of 398.8 km² (154 sq. mi.), and is 154 m (505 ft.) at its deepest point.

One of the **largest concentrations of osprey** in the world is around Kootenay Lake. There are at least one hundred breeding pairs with twenty-five of them on the West Arm alone.

The blue colours in this glacier are awesome and well worth seeing.

There are at least **43 lakes in B.C.** with areas greater than 51.8 km² (20 sq. mi.).

Christina Lake, near Grand Forks, B.C. is called **the warmest lake in B.C.** - however, Osoyoos also claims to have Canada's warmest freshwater lake.

The **highest lake in Canada** is Chilco (or Chilko) Lake B.C. It is located in the Coast Range Mountains east of Mt. Waddington and covers an area of 194.5 km² (75.1 sq. mi.) at an elevation of 1,171 m (3,842 ft.). There are a great many smaller lakes at even higher elevations.

The **Okanagan Lake Floating Bridge** at Kelowna was opened by Princess Margaret in 1958 to replace government ferries. It is the only one of its kind in Canada. The floating portion, 650 m (2,132.5 ft.) long, consists of concrete portions anchored to the bottom of the lake.

The **only inland navigational lock system** in Western Canada is at the Hugh Keenleyside Dam at the south end of Arrow Lake.

Ogopogo of Okanagan Lake. This elusive "serpent" has been seen on many occasions by reliable witnesses, since before the days of the white man. From February 15, 1984 until February 15, 1985 the Okanagan-Similkameen Tourist Association offered a reward of $1,000,000 for positive proof of this friendly monster's existence. The legendary denizen of Okanagan Lake, Ogopogo, is protected by provincial legislation. By having it officially designated as "wildlife," the Wildlife Act prohibits any person from capturing, killing or harassing the creature.

ODDS & ENDS

In 1987 the **Vancouver Aquarium** was designated Canada's Pacific National Aquarium and, in the same year, it received the National Travel and Tourism Award for the top tourist attraction in Canada.

The Vancouver Aquarium is **the largest aquarium in Canada**. It has about 9,600 specimens of 587 species. Of these almost 7,500 are saltwater and the rest freshwater specimens. The Dolphin and Killer Whale shows are no longer regularly scheduled. Under a new program, the daily feeding shows have been replaced by constantly changing exercises and activities. The Aquarium's staff feels that this provides "more mental stimulus and challenge for the whales." The Aquarium is quite pleased with the results.

With about **9,600 live specimens** at the Vancouver Aquarium, births of one kind or another are common. Not so common are births of killer whales in captivity. On September 30, 1991, their female killer whale, Bjossa, gave birth to a female calf. On October 25, Bjossa's milk supply dried up. The baby is now "being fed formula by (aquarium) staff every four hours." Killer whale calves have never been successfully hand-reared before, and even in the wild 50% of all killer whale calves die before they are six months old.

The annual **World Championship Bathtub Race**, 34 miles, between Nanaimo and Vancouver, takes place on the fourth Sunday in July at the end of the 10-day Nanaimo Marine Festival. From a very humble beginning in 1967, it has become one of B.C.'s major international attractions. The longest crossing was the first, in 1967, by Rusty Harrison of Vancouver, in 3:26:00. The fastest time to date is 1:17:47 by Jimmy Dunn of Vancouver, in 1990. There are rules governing the size and shape of the tub; the size and type of engine, the type of fuel used, and how the engine is mounted. *For further information write: Loyal Nanaimo Bathtub Society, P.O. Box 565, Nanaimo, B.C., V9R 5L5.*

There are **more glaciers** in British Columbia than in any other province or state in North America.

WATERFALLS

Of the six highest waterfalls in Canada, five are in B.C.

Takakka Falls	503 m (1,650 ft.)	Daly Glacier, B.C.
Della Falls	440 m (1,444 ft.)	Della Lake, B.C.
Hunlen Falls	253 m (830 ft.)	Atnarko River, B.C.
Panther Falls	183 m (600 ft.)	Nigel Creek, Alberta
Helmcken Fall	137 m (449 ft.)	Murtle River, B.C.
Bridal Veil Falls	122 m (400 ft.)	Bridal Creek, B.C.

SPORT FISHING

In B.C.'s coastal waters there are at least 30 known varieties of starfish, or sea stars, 400 species of seaweed, and over 325 species of fish. The largest octopi in the world live off the coast of B.C. The waters of this province have been rated second only to the Red Sea in richness and variety of its underwater life. For divers the coastal waters are clearest between October and March when visibility is between 20 and 30 m (65 to 100 ft.).

On the average, about 300,000 freshwater **sportfishing licences** are sold to residents and 90,000 to non-residents.

There are at least seventy species and subspecies of **freshwater fish** in B.C. waters.

The Fraser River is the **major migratory route** for Pacific salmon.

There are 143 species of mammals, 19 species of reptiles, and 20 species of amphibians found in and around B.C. waters.

There are at least **11 species of shark** known in B.C. waters, including the notorious "Great White". There have been no known attacks on swimmers in B.C. waters but experts feel that such incidents are inevitable with the appearance of more dangerous species due, in part, to the warm Japanese Current which splits off the Oregon coast and flows up off B.C. to Alaska.

The largest fly fishing rod in the world is at Houston, B.C. It is 18.3 m (60 ft.) in length with a 53.3 cm (21 in.) fly. The rod is anodized aluminum and the fly is a florescent "Skykomish Sunrise."

Garry Oling of Maple Ridge, B.C. got into the Guinness Book of World Records for catching, or lassoing, a 378.3 kg (834 lb.) **giant sturgeon** in the Fraser River. With some help he pulled it about half a mile (805 m) to the nearest dock before he could get it out.

In 1932 a trout described as weighing 25.4 kg (56 lbs.) was caught in Jewel Lake (N.E. of Greenwood). It is **the largest trout** ever to be caught by hook and line.

The **largest rainbow trout** in the world are found in the Lardeau River.

The **largest rainbow trout** ever caught in Kootenay Lake weighed in at 16.2 kg (35.75lbs.). It was caught in the Gray Creek area. Dolly Varden and kokanee are also in abundance.

B.C.'s Cariboo - Chilcotin areas have **over 4,000 lakes** which support rainbow, kokanee, lake trout, Dolly Varden, eastern brook trout and coastal cutthroat.

Merritt and the Nicola Valley is a **fisherman's paradise**. Their boast is "A lake a day as long as you stay."

The **largest Coho (Silver) salmon** ever caught on sport tackle weighed 14.3 g (31.5 lbs.). It was caught in Cowichan Bay by Mrs. Lee Hallberg on October 11, 1947.

July 19, 1959 —The **largest Chinook salmon** ever caught in B.C. was 41.7 kg (92 lbs.) in weight, 148.6 cm (58.5 in.) in length awith a girth of 91.4 cm (36 in.). It was caught in the Skeena River by Heinz Wichmann. The world record Chinook was 57.2 kg (126 lbs.), 134.6 cm (53 in.) long and caught at Petersburg, Alaska in 1948.

A California fisherman, while fishing more than 10 miles out into the Pacific from Ucluelet, **accidentally dropped his wallet** overboard. A month or so later he received his wallet in the mail with its contents intact. It had been found some 20 miles away on Long Beach.

CHAPTER 13

CITIES & TOWNS

The town of Atlin, on the east shore of Atlin Lake, is considered to be B.C.'s **most remote outpost.**

During the 1860s Barkerville was **the largest town**, by population, north of San Francisco and west of Chicago.

Centreville, population two, claims to be **the smallest community** in B.C. It was a gold rush town of 3,000 in the 1870s.

The **downtown revitalization project** of Chemainus became an "internationally famous success" with the introduction of a series of enormous murals throughout the downtown area depicting the history of the Chemainus area. This unique idea gives them the nickname of "The Little Town That Did."

The town of Clayburn, in the lower Fraser Valley (near Abbotsford), was **the first "company town"** in B.C. It was settled in 1905 because of the good brickmaking quality of the clay in the area. The Vancouver Fireclay Company built most of the buildings and controlled all of the utilities serving the town.

From 1910 to 1920 Cumberland had the **second largest Chinatown** in North America. Today, Vancouver's Chinatown is second only to that of San Francisco.

In 1983, Duncan, the first city in the province to complete a downtown revitalization project, became the **"City of Totems."** Mayor Doug Barker came up with the idea of lining the city's approaches on Highway No. 1 with totem poles. The rest is history.

Fort Nelson, established in 1805 as a supply centre, sprang into prominence with the building of the Alaska Highway. It is **now a major centre** and stopping place along that route.

Fort St. James is **B.C.'s oldest established community.** (185 years old in 1991), and also claims to be the oldest white settlement on B.C.'s mainland.

Kelowna is at the centre of the **largest fruit growing area** in Canada and a third of all its fruit shipments originate here.

The Canadian Encyclopedia shows the City of Kimberley to be at an elevation of 1,120 m (3,675 ft.) which would make it the **highest city in Canada.**

The name **Lillooet** is an Native word which means "wild onion."

An 1868 photo of Barkerville before the fire.

Vancouver in 1927.

In 1961 the village of Masset became the **first town to be incorporated** on the Queen Charlotte Islands.

Moricetown is **B.C.'s oldest community**. It has been a Carrier village site for over 5,000 years. It is located in the Bulkley Valley area of B.C., between Smithers and New Hazelton.

Nelson was the first city in B.C. **to operate an electric power plant**. (on Cottonwood Creek). Nelson was the smallest city in Canada to have a streetcar system, which ran from 1899 to 1949. Parts of it were to become operational again in 1991.

On July 16, 1860 New Westminster was incorporated as a municipality and was the first town in B.C. to be granted such a proclamation. It is the **first incorporated municipality** west of the Great Lakes. New Westminster is also known as "The Royal City."

"In God We Trust." These words, I am sure, will be familiar to most people from U.S. coins. They first appeared on an American two-cent piece in 1864. The Coat of Arms of the City of New Westminster also carries these words. The city's crest was designed by Col. Moody of the Royal Engineers and presented to the New Westminster Municipal Council on Nov. 10, 1860.

Prince George is the **trade, commerce and cultural centre** of northern B.C. With a population of 70,000 it is a city with many attractions, including 116 parks within the city limits. There are numerous festivals and cultural events throughout the year to attract people from all walks of life. Its prime industry is forestry and the major operator in this field is Northwood Pulp and Timber. Their pulp mill is one of the largest in the world. A tour of Northwood's facilities usually takes three hours.

Prince Rupert's harbour is one of the **largest ice-free ports** in the world and caters to hundreds of deep-sea vessels from all over the globe.

The Canadian World Almanac, 1989, shows Rossland, B.C. as being the **highest city in Canada** at 1,056 m (3,465 ft.).

Smithers was founded in 1913 as the divisional headquarters for the Grand Trunk Pacific Railway (now the CNR). It then became the **first incorporated village** in B.C. The downtown area has a Bavarian atmosphere.

Stewart, B.C., Canada's most **northerly ice free port** is connected to Hyder, Alaska, the southernmost town in Alaska, by a highway. Both communities are located at the head of Portland Canal, which is the fourth largest fjord in the world.

The **second largest municipality** in B.C., Surrey, is 324 km² (125.1 sq. mi.) in size, and is also the fastest growing municipality by population.

Terrace had its beginning as a firewood stop for the paddlewheelers on the Skeena River.

The Kermodei Bear has been adopted by the City of Terrace as its official "corporate identity" and is on its corporate seal. The Kermodei Bear, a white bear found only in the Terrace area and on Princess Royal Island, was named after Francis Kermode, a director of the B.C. Provincial Museum in the early 1900s. His early efforts at securing specimens and information on them eventually resulted in provincial regulations protecting the species.

The town of Three Valley Gap combines a modern resort with a historic town. The site was first noted by Walter Moberly on Aug. 29, 1865 when he discovered Eagle Pass for the CPR. Three Valley Gap was a boom town in the 1880s with the building of the railway. It almost died out until the late 1950s when Gordon and Ethel Bell decided to rebuild and restore it. Today it consists of over twenty historic buildings collected from around B.C., along with its modern 103 room motel and amenities. The town is located 19 km (11.8 mi.) west of Revelstoke on the Trans Canada Highway.

The newest, and also **largest, municipality in B.C.** was formed in 1982. Tumbler Ridge, the "Instant Town," was designed to serve the needs of the rapidly developing northeast coal mines. Surrey was formerly the largest but now has been reduced to second place in both population and area.

The **City of Vancouver** was formed from three small settlements: Granville, Gastown and Hastings Mill.

Sir William Van Horne, a Dutch-American, was responsible for **building the Canadian Pacific Railway** westward to Vancouver. Van Horne, who afterwards became chairman and president of the railway company, first suggested naming the city after George Vancouver, one of the world's greatest navigators, who also was of Dutch ancestry.

The **narrowest building in the world** is on Pender Street in Vancouver, according to Ripley's Believe It Or Not. It is 1.5 m (4.9 ft.) wide and 29 m (95 ft.) long.

The **oldest building in Vancouver** is the Hastings Mill Store Museum. Built at Hastings in 1865, it was moved by barge to its present location, at the north foot of Alma Street, in 1930.

On April 27, 1986 there was a peace march and rally at B.C. Place Stadium in Vancouver. It was from this they called Vancouver **"The Peace Capital of North America."**

Maybe this is one reason why the area is known as "The Valley of the Ghosts."

The **total amount of garbage** produced per year in the Greater Vancouver area is over 1 megaton. This is enough to over-fill BC Place Stadium right to its roof.

Vanderhoof, besides being located at the **geographical centre of the province**, also considers itself the "recreational centre" of British Columbia. There are four major celebrations during the year including the rodeo which "is held in the largest indoor rodeo ring in the north," and the Vanderhoof International Airshow, the second largest airshow in B.C. The nearby Nechako Bird Sanctuary is home to 50,000 Canada Geese in the spring and fall.

Vernon is the **oldest city in the interior** and the fifth oldest in the province. Vernon was incorporated in 1892.

A fall, 1989 edition of *Condé Nast Traveler* magazine places Victoria among the **top ten cities** in the world to visit. It is estimated Victoria has almost three million visitors annually. (Vancouver is 19th on the list.)

One of the **narrowest streets in Canada** is Fan Tan Alley in Victoria's Chinatown. It is about 1.5 m (5 ft.) wide.

The town of Westbank, B.C. is the only Okanagan community to be marked with a cairn by the Historic Sites and Monuments Board of Canada. Its plaque tells the **story of the fur trade** dating back to 1811. The monument itself is made of basalt from Mount Boucherie.

Williams Lake, B.C., has an **official civic holiday** not enjoyed by any other community. It is called Wrestling Day and it is celebrated the day after New Years in the same way Boxing Day is celebrated the day after Christmas. Provincial offices are closed; however, federal offices and banks remain open.

MOTTOS AND SLOGANS

A lot of B.C. communities have a motto, slogan, nickname, or whatever. Some of them are very good, descriptive and/or enlightening. Some have had these mottos for a long time, e.g. "The Royal City," while a lot of others were created for the Expo year of 1986. Some places have more than one and some places don't have them or use them if they do.

Abbotsford is "Hub of the Fraser Valley."

Agassiz is "Corn Capital of B.C."

Aldergrove has "Country Style Hospitality."

Alert Bay is "Home of the Killer Whale."

Armstrong is the "Celery City of B.C."

Ashcroft is "Sun Country."

Burnaby is "The Centre of it all."

Cache Creek claims "We Knew We Could — And Did."

Campbell River is the "Reel Salmon Fishing Capital of the World."

Chemainus is "The Little Town that Did."

Clearbrook, Abbotsford and Matsqui all claim to be the "Raspberry Capital of Canada."

Coalmont (1911) was "The City of Destiny."

Coldstream is "Rural Living at its Best."

Comox Valley is the "All Seasons Resort."

Coquitlam is "Home of the Dogwood."

Creston is "The Apple of the Kootenays."

Dawson Creek is "Mile '0' City" (start of Alaska Highway).

Deas Lake calls itself "The Jade Capital of the Province."

Delta says "Delta Accommodates."

Duncan is the "City of Totems" and is also the "Warm Heart of the Cowichan Valley."

Elkford is the "Wilderness Capital of B.C."

Esquimalt is the "Place of Shoaling Waters."

Fernie is the "Outdoor Capital of B.C."

Fort St. John is the "Energy Capital."

Gabriola is called "Queen of the Islands" or "Nanaimo's Little Island" or "Petroglyph Island" (because of its rock carvings).

Gold River is the "Caving Capital of Canada" and also the "Gateway to Historic Nootka Sound."

Houston is the "Steelhead Capital of the World."

Canada Place in Vancouver.

Kamloops was (1911) "The Los Angeles of Canada."

Kelowna is "Canada's Apple Capital" and "City of Sun, Sand and Smiles" and "The City of all Seasons."

Keremeos is the "Fruit Stand Capital of Canada."

Kimberley is the "Bavarian City of the Rockies."

Kitimat is the "Aluminum City."

Lac la Hache calls itself the "Longest Town in the Cariboo."

Ladner is the "Daffodil Capital of Canada."

Ladysmith is "On the 49th Parallel."

Lake Cowichan is the "Recreation Capital of the Cowichan Valley."

Langley offers "Country Style Hospitality."

Lillooet is "British Columbia's Little Nugget."

Lumby is the "Gateway to the Monashee."

Lytton is the "Rafting Capital of Canada."

Maple Ridge is "Mountain Magic."

Matsqui is "The World's Berry Capital."

Metchosen is "The New Municipality."

Mill Bay is the "Gateway to the Cowichan Valley."

Mission is "Where Mountain Meets Meadow" and the "Shake and Shingle Capital of Canada."

Nanaimo is the "Harbour City."

Nelson is the "Queen City of the Kootenays" and the "Heritage Capital of B.C."

New Denver is "The Lucerne of North America."

New Westminster is "The Royal City."

Okanagan Falls calls itself the "Flea Market Capital of Canada."

Oliver is the "Cantaloupe City of B.C."

100 Mile House is the "Friendliest Town in the Cariboo."

Osoyoos is the "Spanish Capital of Canada."

Parksville has "The Beach at our Doorstep."

Peachland is "Our Place in the Sun."

Pemberton is the scenic "Gateway to Adventure."

Penticton is the "Hospitality Capital of Canada" and is also the "Square Dance Capital of Canada."

Port Alberni is the "Forestry Capital of Canada" and also the "Salmon Capital of the World."

Port Alice is "Where History and Nature Abound."

Port Hardy is "King Coho Country."

Port McNeill is the "Hub of Northern Vancouver Island."

Port Moody is the "Hand Car Capital of the World."

Prince George is the "White Spruce Capital of the World."

Prince Rupert is the "City of Rainbows," the "Gateway to Northern Adventure," the "Halibut Capital of the World" and "Home of the Great Race."

Qualicum Beach is "Vancouver Island's Best Kept Secret."

Quesnel is the "Gold Pan City."

Richmond is the "Gateway to the Pacific."

Rossland is the "Golden City."

Saanich is "Home of Butchart Gardens."

Sayward is the "Best Little Logging Town in Canada."

Sayward and Kelsey Bay are known as "The Valley of a Thousand Faces."

Shuswap Lake is the "Houseboating Capital of B.C."

Sidney is "Where Sea and Sunshine Meet."

Smithers is "Where Alpine Hospitality Peaks."

Sparwood is the "Clean Coal Capital of the World."

Spuzzum is the "Smallest and Friendliest Town in the West."

Squamish is "Home of Gary Baldy" and is "Sea to Sky Country."

Summerland is "British Columbia's Best Kept Secret."

Surrey is "The Best of Both Worlds."

Tahsis is "Home of the Great Walk."

Terrace is "Home of the Kermodei Bear."

Tofino hopes you "Enjoy Your Stay."

Trail is the "Silver City."

Ucluelet is the "Whale Watching Capital of the World."

Vancouver is the "Traffic Jam Capital of Canada." It is also the "Peace Capital of North America," the "Graffiti capital of Canada" and "The World in a City."

Victoria is the "City of Gardens" and is the "Most English City in North America."

Whistler is "B.C.'s Year Round Mountain Resort."

White Rock is the "Sandcastle Capital of the World."

Williams Lake is the "Stampede Capital — Hub of the Cariboo."

Zeballos is the "Site of Vancouver Island's only Gold Rush."

MISCELLANEOUS NAMES

The north-west corner of B.C. has been called **"The Switzerland of North America."**

Highway 31A from New Denver to Kaslo winds through **"The Valley of the Ghosts."** So named from the fact that in the 1890s several towns and dozens of towns which flourished in the area. Now there is hardly any indication at all of their presence or former prominence.

During those "boomtown" days of the late 1800s and early 1900s this same area was known as the **"Silvery Slocan"** due to the abundance of this metal in the surrounding hills.

The sign at the entrance to Spuzzum declares it "The Smallest and Friendliest Town in the West." Small? Yes. The sign in the lower left corner declares that you are now leaving Spuzzum.

The Kootenay Lake Valley is known as the **"Valley of the Swans."** At the south end of the lake is the Creston Valley Wildlife Interpretation Centre over which a quarter of a million game birds pass annually. Peak migration periods are around mid-March in the spring and during October in the fall.

The area in and around Chilliwack, Cultus, Harrison, Aggassiz, and Hope is known as **"Rainbow Country."**

Highway 37A from Meziadin Junction to Stewart is called **"The Glacier Highway to Alaska."**

When the town of Okanagan Falls was formed, it was called, with high hopes, **"The Queen City of the Okanagan."** There are no falls at Okanagan Falls.

QUIZ OF PLACE NAMES IN B.C.

From the brief clues below, name 50 towns in B.C.
Answers on page 88.
All names taken from British Columbia Road Map and Parks Guide 1991-92.

1. Birds cry and a weight
2. Unseasoned timber
3. Fat body of water
4. Bill's water
5. A path in the woods
6. Go to first base
7. A mulligan and a drawing
8. A great Queen
9. On a flat world the
10. Type of lock
11. Diet Pepsi I hope
12. A canopy
13. ____ Impossible
14. Very possible
15. Hard to drive here
16. What a Blacksmith needs
17. Little over a hundred
18. Writing tool, clock sound, weight
19. Evening flatland
20. A bird's home
21. Springs Eternal
22. A feline carpet
23. Newly wedded female's town
24. A praiseworthy feature
25. Beach area
26. Magnificent cutlery
27. A waterfall
28. Underground water supply
29. Dog sent for big animal
30. A big throw
31. Getting ahead or making
32. Fishy part of the body
33. A Monk's car
34. A New England pub
35. ____ and pins
36. Exchanging moccasins
37. First man's body of water
38. Royal entrance
39. Expensive teeth
40. A cold slap
41. Sugar makers bridge bid
42. Maker of garments
43. Wine and cantaloupe
44. Raised level ground
45. Amazing sandy area
46. A tardy container
47. A watchful body of water
48. Charles' weight
49. Ice cream and fix the fire
50. Point of no return
51. How many islands are there in the Queen Charlotte Islands?
52. How high are the falls at Okanagan Falls?
53. For whom was Fort Alexandria named?
54. Where is the "Fraser" customs post?
55. There are two "Heritage Parks" in B.C. What or where are they?
56. The second weekend of August is the annual Filomi Days celebration at Port Hardy, on Vancouver Island. What does "Filomi" mean?
57. Name two rivers which start in B.C. and flow through the U.S. before emptying into the sea?

CHAPTER 14

PARKS

Total parkland in B.C.: National, provincial, regional, and ecological reserves equals 5,955,949 ha or about 6.28 % of the province's total area. (59,559.5 km²) This is greater than the province of Nova Scotia.

NATIONAL PARKS

The **purpose of the National Parks** are to "preserve the best examples of the Canadian natural environment and to allow the natural processes to go on as freely as possible." National Parks have "Interpreter Service Programs" which are designed to increase visitors' enjoyment of the park's natural heritage.

There are **six National Parks** in British Columbia and four National Historic Parks and Sites.

National Parks in B.C. cover 970,600 hectares (2,398,320 acres).

In **Yoho National Park** there are about 30 peaks with heights of 3,050 m+ (10,000 ft.)

A sign at the west entrance to **Kootenay National Park** declares: "The Mountains Shall Bring Peace To The People." In plain English "If you wish to exult in the ecstatic experience of being enchantingly exiled in a satisfying setting of the serenity, symmetry and stateliness, go to the mountains" — John O.A. Peets.

Canada's **first National Marine Park**, the Pacific Rim National Park, was established in 1970 on the west coast of Vancouver Island. It consists of three geographically separate units: Long Beach, the Broken Group Islands (at the entrance to Barkley Sound), and the West Coast Trail (one of the toughest five-day hikes in Canada).

Kootenay National Park is the only National Park in Canada where it is possible to find **both glaciers and cacti**.

Canada's **33rd National Park** was established in July of 1987 on the South Moresby Island area of the Queen Charlotte Islands. The Haida claim this as a victory in their struggle against the federal and provincial governments to preserve the area and stop commercial logging on the land they claim belongs to them.

South Moresby, in the Queen Charlotte Islands, is used by more than **30% of British Columbia's nesting seabirds**. This area is also thought to have the second highest bald eagle nesting density in the world.

Of the 73 Historic Parks and Sites in Canada, **six are in British Columbia:** Fort Langley (est. 1924), Fort Rodd Hill (1962), Fisgard Lighthouse (1962), St. Roch (1974), Fort St. James (1977) and Kitwanga Fort (1985).

A sign at the entrance to Kootenay National Park.

B.C. NATIONAL PARKS

The six National Parks in B.C. are:

Glacier
established 1886   1,349 km²

Kootenay
established 1920   1,406 km²

Mt. Revelstoke
established 1914   263 km²

Pacific Rim
established 1970   511 km²

South Moresby Reserve*
established 1987   4,864 km²

Yoho
established 1886   1,313 km²

The South Moresby National Park Reserve consists of 1,470 km² land area, and the South Moresby National Marine Park Reserve has a further 3,394 km² of marine environment. The fact it is called a "reserve" simply means its boundaries have not yet been firmly established but could soon be increased to full park status.

Fisgard Lighthouse National Historic Site located at Fort Rodd Hill, Victoria, was the **first permanent lighthouse** on the rugged west coast of Canada. It is still in operation today.

The **R.C.M.P. vessel St. Roch**, now a National Historic Site in Vancouver, made four important maritime firsts. In June. 1940 she left Vancouver heading for Halifax via the Northwest Passage. She was the first ship to complete this route, taking 28 months. The return trip was the first east to west passage, from Halifax to Vancouver, and the first passage in a single season (July 22, 1944 - Oct. 16, 1944). In 1950 she returned to Halifax from Vancouver, via the Panama Canal and thus became the first ship to completely circumnavigate the North American continent.

In 1806, Simon Fraser built the **first fort in B.C.** for the Hudson Bay Company. Today this site, at Fort St. James, is a National Historic Park. It is located less than an hour's drive north of Vanderhoof in the very centre of B.C., and is an authentic Hudson Bay Trading Post, complete with staff in period costumes. Admission is free.

The concentrator of the Britannia Mine, at Britannia Beach, B.C., has been designated or recognized as a National Historic Site by the Historic Sites and Monuments Board of Canada. The British Columbia Museum of Mining is also located here.

Port Edward, B.C., 20 minutes south of Prince Rupert, is the site of the **"Oldest Surviving Salmon Cannery in British Columbia."** It was built in 1889 and was one of about 200 on the west coast of B.C. It closed in 1968. Today "North Pacific" is an authentic cannery village and museum, and was declared a National Historic Site in 1985 by both the federal and provincial governments.

PROVINCIAL PARKS

Provincial Parks are **areas of land set aside by provincial governments,** within their own jurisdiction, for the "conservation of the natural environment and the enjoyment of residents and visitors" alike.

There are **385 Provincial Parks** in B.C. covering 5,364,501 ha (13,255,500 acres). This is equivalent to 5.66% of the province's total area. About half of these parks have campgrounds containing a total of 11,429 campsites.

B.C. has the **largest provincial or state park system** in North America, covering an area the size of Nova Scotia. Almost 80% of this is in Class A parks.

Over 170 of British Columbia's parks provide sites for daytime recreation.

One out of every ten provincial parks in British Columbia is "a wilderness, largely untouched and frequented mostly by back-packers and mountaineers."

*"A Giant Among Trees —You are standing beneath what is perhaps the largest Yellow Cedar in the world! Estimated at 40 m (150 ft.) tall and 9 m (29 ft.) around the trunk, this slow growing tree began its life as a seed over 1,000 years ago. Its size is amazing as there are only 130 frost-free days a year (average) and snowpack reaches 3.5 - 4.0 m (12 -15 ft.) at this elevation.
It's hard to imagine this tree was over 500 years old when Columbus reached America.*

Over **20 million people per year** visit provincial parks in B.C.

The **first provincial park in B.C.** was Strathcona Provincial Park, on Vancouver Island, and it was established in 1911.

Tweedsmuir Provincial Park is **the largest in B.C.** It was named for the 15th Governor General of Canada, John Buchan, first Baron of Tweedsmuir, who once said "I have now travelled over most of Canada and have seen many wonderful things, but I have seen nothing more beautiful and more wonderful than the great park which British Columbia has done me the honour to call by my name."

Lonesome Lake, made famous by Ralph Edwards through his stories of pioneering, homesteading and conservation, and by his efforts to protect the trumpeter swan, is located in Tweedsmuir Provincial Park south of Highway 20.

B.C.'s **smallest provincial park** is Deadman's Island, in Burns Lake.

Spatsizi Plateau Wilderness Park is considered one of the **most important wildlife parks** in Canada. It is not accessible by road and is home to some of the largest remaining herds of Osborne caribou, stone sheep, moose, wolves and grizzly bear.

Mount Edziza Park is one of the **most impressive recent volcanic areas** in B.C. Mount Edziza itself has a glacier filled crater surrounded by numerous cinder cones and lava beds. It is not accessible by road.

Mount Edziza Park, west of the Cassiar Highway (No. 37), and Spatsizi Park, east of the Cassiar Highway, are joined by a 10 km (6.2 mi.) wide strip of land along the Stikine River which crosses the Cassiar Highway.

The only established **freshwater scuba diving park** in B.C. is on the northeastern shore of Okanagan Lake at Ellison Provincial Park near Vernon. Also located in this park are six archaeological sites.

Cody Caves - Discovered in the 1890s by prospector Henry Cody, these caves were carved out of limestone about 170 million years ago by water seeping through cracks in the rock. The limestone itself was formed about 600 million years ago on an ancient ocean floor. To protect the cave from damage by curiosity seekers, the provincial government created the Cody Caves Provincial Park in 1965 and gave it a "Class A" status. The caves are accessible from Highway 31 just north of Ainsworth Hot Springs.

The **Purcell Wilderness Conservancy** in the East Kootenay is the first such preserve in B.C. Basically, a wilderness conservancy is a park in which there are no roads, buildings, or motor vehicles of any type allowed at any time. There are trails for hikers and the rules are strictly adhered to.

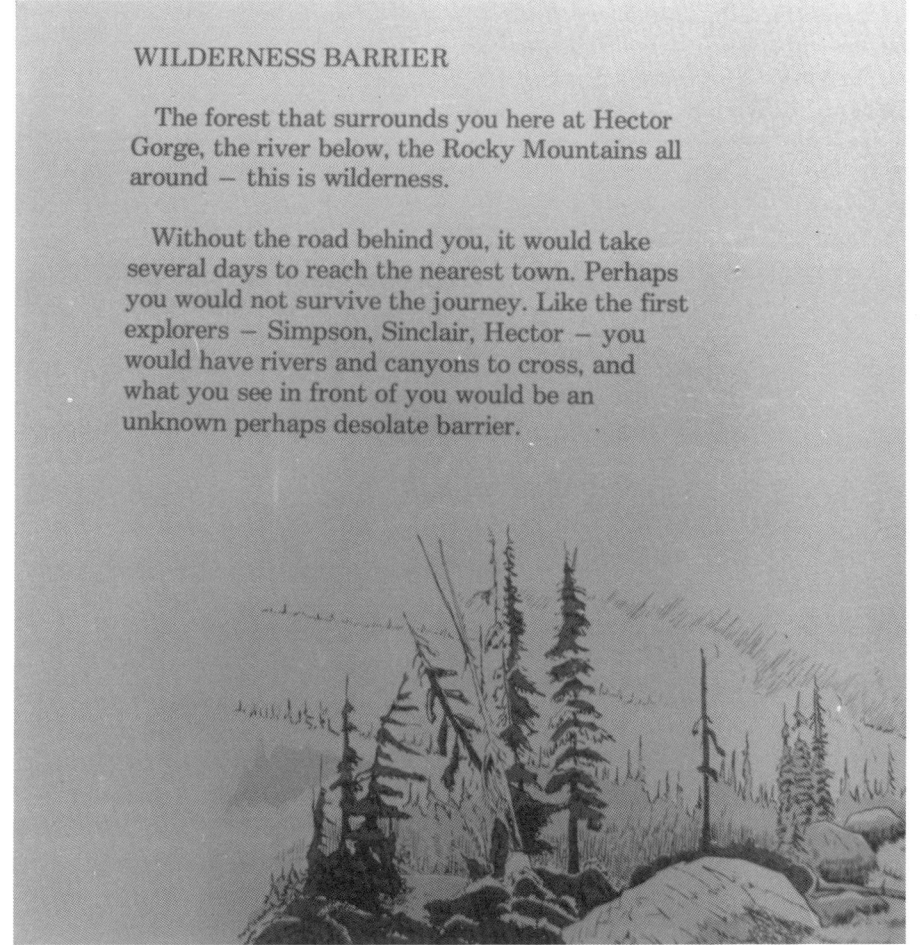

WILDERNESS BARRIER

The forest that surrounds you here at Hector Gorge, the river below, the Rocky Mountains all around — this is wilderness.

Without the road behind you, it would take several days to reach the nearest town. Perhaps you would not survive the journey. Like the first explorers — Simpson, Sinclair, Hector — you would have rivers and canyons to cross, and what you see in front of you would be an unknown perhaps desolate barrier.

You can get an idea of the natural richness of the Queen Charlotte Islands at the Delkatla Wildlife Sanctuary where **113 different species of birds** have been sighted and recorded.

Ecological reserves (land only) in B.C. cover an area of 107,321 ha (265,187 acres).

Regional, or municipal, parks in B.C. cover 8,128 ha (20,084 acres) of land.

The **University Endowment Lands**, in Vancouver, were designated as a park in perpetuity by the B.C. Provincial Government. This now makes the 2,100-acre site one of the largest urban parks in the world. (Compare this to other world famous parks, such as: Stanley Park in Vancouver at 1,000 acres; Mount Royal Park in Montréal at 494 acres; Central Park in New York at 840 acres; and Hyde Park in London, England at 615 acres.)

Stanley Park, in Vancouver, has **more visitors per year** than any other park in B.C. Bear Creek Park in Surrey is second.

The line of B.C.'s Lower Mainline Rapid Transit System is also the site of a 50 acre linear park which parallels the system through Vancouver, Burnaby and New Westminster. Called **"B.C. Parkway,"** it has a walking and bicycling path along its length.

There are 116 parks within the City of Prince George.

The Wild & Wet Waterslide Park's **"Ravine River Ride,"** just south of Kelowna, "offers 700 feet of spills, splashes, thrills and fun..." It is the longest slide of its kind in Canada. This water park is one of the largest in Western Canada.

The **largest living Sitka Spruce tree** in B.C. is growing in Radley Park in Kitimat.

CHAPTER 15

ARTS & ENTERTAINMENT

THE ARTS

Fairs & Festivals

The largest fair in B.C. is the Pacific National Exhibition (PNE) in Vancouver. It is preceded by the largest parade in the province.

The **second largest fair** in B.C. is the Interior Provincial Exhibition (IPE), which is held in Armstrong.

The **second largest annual parade** in B.C. is the "Peach Festival Parade" in Penticton.

THE GLASS HOUSE

Overlooking Kootenay Lake at Boswell is one of the most unique houses in B.C. It is made of 500,000 empty embalming fluid bottles. After 35 years in the funeral business, David H. Brown retired in 1952 and decided to build a home out of all these bottles, which he had collected from all over Western Canada. Although meant to be his home, the project became an instant tourist attraction and now includes a glass bottle bridge and pathways bordered by at least 120 dozen flowers. Tours from May to October.

The New Westminster Hyack Festival began as May Day in 1870 and has been an annual event since that time. It is **one of B.C.'s largest festivals**.

Music

During the 1980s the Vancouver Symphony had some 40,000 subscribers, confirmed by National Geographic as the **largest subscription audience** of any orchestra in the world.

The **largest rock concert** in B.C. was Michael Jackson's "Victory Tour" at B.C. Place Stadium, November 16, 17 and 18, 1984. Total attendance was about 110,000.

Bryan Adams, of North Vancouver, is one of the **most successful Canadian "rockers"** in history.

Bryan Adams' new single "Everything I do (I do for you)" was on the top of the British pop music charts for **12 consecutive weeks** in 1991. This broke the previous record of 11 weeks which had been set with "Rose Marie" by Slim Whitman in 1955.

Bryan Adams' first album in four years is considered by some to be a classic. "Waking up the Neighbours," unfortu-

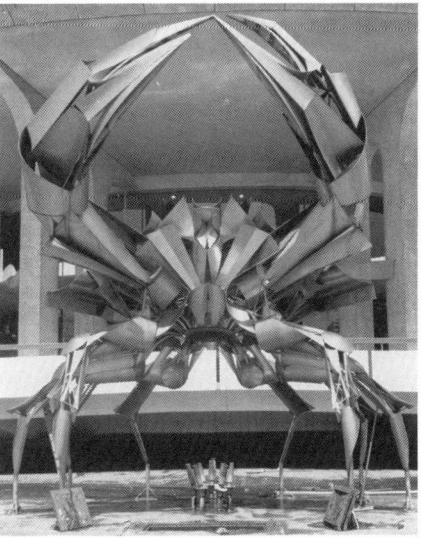

"The Crab" at the Vacouver Planetarium. This fountain sculpture, made by George Norris, was commisioned by the Women's Activities Group of the Centennial Committee of Vancouver as a gift to the citzens of Vancouver.

nately, was recorded in England; the CRTC therefore says Bryan is now **not a Canadian** (at least for this album) and it won't allow any radio station to play it more than 19 times a week.

Pat Hobbis of Nanaimo set a new world record for the **longest continuous drum solo**. After 45 days, from Aug 17 to Oct. 1, 1985, he officially ended his marathon, which surpassed the old record by three days.

Odds & Ends

Located near Sayward, B.C., is the **Valley of a Thousand Faces**. This is a parklike forest area "where 1,000 faces painted on cedar slabs hang on trees." The faces include many well known people, natives from around the world, and famous cartoon characters. A walkway through the area is enhanced with a variety of flowers and is a "wonderful and unique experience."

The **oldest tourist bureau** in North America is the Vancouver Convention and Visitors Bureau. It was formed in 1918.

The **oldest continuously held event** in British Columbia is the Clinton Ball. It has been an annual event since 1868 and is usually held in May.

The **largest indoor summer theatre** in B.C. is the Wildhorse Theatre at Fort Steele. During the summer, live vaudeville stage shows are presented in this rebuilt turn-of-the-century theatre. The town itself is an Historic Park of the 1890-1905 era.

"The Gate to the North-West Passage by Chung Hung.

English novelist Malcolm Lowry lived in Canada from 1939 to 1954, mostly in a squatter's shack in Dollarton, now part of Greater Vancouver, where he worked on his classic novel *Under the Volcano*.

Every August Penticton hosts the huge **British Columbia Square Dance Jamboree**. Originating in 1954, it is a week-long affair drawing up to 10,000 participants and spectators from all over North America. From this Penticton has acquired the title "Square Dance Capital of Canada." This event takes place on the world's largest outdoor dance floor, almost 0.4 ha (1 acre) in size, located in King's Park.

The **"Ksan Indian Village and Museum"** is a world famous Northwest Coast Native Cultural Centre. It has been open for over twenty years and is a combination museum, Native wood carving school, gift shop and cultural centre. It is located near Hazleton on Highway 16.

The **Mission Pow Wow**, an annual event in Mission, B.C., draws entrants from all over North America. Natives in full dress costumes compete in a variety of events for many cash prizes.

Chief Dan George, of the Squamish band, was one of B.C.'s **most famous**

This photo of a black bear was taken in Adams Igloo. It is part of a $300,000 collection of stuffed North American birds and animals.

natives. Besides being chief of his band, he was also a longshoreman, a logger, an actor, a writer, a public speaker and an environmentalist.

The **largest collection of grizzly bears** in North America resides in Adams Igloo, a few minutes north of Smithers on Highway 16. On display are full size specimens of all of the big game animals in British Columbia, other fur bearers and birds. All are life-sized and mounted in a scenic wooded area setting. It's very impressive.

A set of diesel horns on top of the B.C. Hydro building in Vancouver plays the first four notes of **"O Canada"** everyday at noon.

Actor Raymond Burr of *Perry Mason* and *Ironside* fame was born in New Westminster in 1917.

Movies

The **first permanent movie house** to be built in Canada, opened in Vancouver in 1902. It was the Edison Electric located on Cordova Street.

The **first talking movie** in Vancouver was shown on October 20, 1928. Its title was "Mother Knows Best."

Movies and TV shows "Made in B.C." are a common occurrence throughout the province. I hesitate to list them all here for fear of inadvertently omitting anyone.

EXPO '86

The **full title** of this fair was "The 1986 World Exposition."

The **17-storey high** (46.2 m or 152 ft.) Expo Centre opened May 2, 1985 as a prelude to Expo '86. It attracted 600,000 visitors, which was double the projected figures and an indication of what was to come. It also contained the World's Largest Omnimax Theatre.

Expo '86 was the **86th World's Fair,** the 46th World's Fair this century, the 24th World's Fair in North America and the 18th this century in North America. The last time Canada hosted the World's Fair was in 1967 at Montreal.

In 1986, during Expo '86, Vancouver celebrated its **100th birthday**. It was also the 150th anniversary of Canadian passenger rail service, the 100th anniversary of trans-continental rail service, the DC-3's 50th anniversary and the 25th year of human space travel.

Expo '86 was held on a **70 ha (173 acre) site** along False Creek in Vancouver.

Prince Charles officially declared Expo '86 open May 2, 1986.

Diana, Princess of Wales, fainted at the California Pavilion during her tour of Expo '86.

Expo '86 had **54 international participants**, the largest number ever to appear at a specialized World Exposition.

The **first country** to agree to become a participant in Expo '86 was Great Britain on April 17, 1981.

The **smallest country** represented at Expo '86 was Nauru.

The **country coming the furthest** to Expo '86 was Sri Lanka.

Norway was the only nation to have **two pavilions** at Expo '86.

The **largest pavilion** ever erected at a World Exposition was the Canada Pavilion at Expo '86.

Canadian Pacific was the **first private corporation** to announce its participation in Expo '86. CP has participated in world expositions since 1893.

Vancouver architect Peter Cardew was presented with the **Award of Excellence** in the 1985 Canadian Architect Awards Program for his design of the CN Pavilion for Expo '86.

Expo '86 had about **15,000 full-time staff members** working on the site and a further 15,000 volunteers.

Expo '86 had a **staff turnover of 70%**. In all, some 37,000 people worked for Expo.

Besides English and French, Expo '86 tour guides spoke a **total of 33 languages.**

Expo's **street entertainment** program consisted of over 800 performers and 150 groups.

Expo's **first aid staff** treated over 80,000 people, mostly for headaches and blisters.

The **clean-up crew** for the Expo grounds went through 1,500 brooms during the 5 1/2 month event.

EXPO TIMELINE

May 2	Expo opened
May 11	It took Expo just 10 days to record its one millionth visitor.
June 17	five million visitors
July 25	ten million visitors
Aug. 20	the original projection of 13,750,000 visitors was broken.
Oct. 4	twenty million visitors
Oct. 12	largest single day attendance: 341,806 visitors
Oct. 13	Expo closed total attendance: 22,111,578 visitors

There were **55 tons of garbage** collected every day at Expo '86.

There were **2,072 rolls of toilet paper** used every day at Expo.

Over **4,000 lost children** were reunited with their parents during Expo '86. (The Vancouver Sun Oct. 12 1986 says 4,071; the Vancouver Province Oct. 10 1986 says 4,134; and the Vancouver Sun of Oct. 14 1986 says 4,087.) Almost 600 disoriented adults also checked into the lost and found department.

Of the **thousands of articles** turned in to Expo's Lost and Found, the most common thing was ID cards.

Items to be seen at Expo's **lost and found department** included cameras, keys, wallets, watches, umbrellas, sunglasses, eye-glasses, false teeth, hearing aids, a wheelchair, a pair of crutches, and various types of clothing.

Expo '86 had the **world's tallest freestanding flag pole** at 86 m (282 ft.) and also the world's largest flag, which flew atop Canada Place. It was 24.4 m x 12.2 m (80 ft. x 40 ft.).

The Swiss Pavilion at Expo '86 had the **world's largest wrist watch**, known as a "swatch."

At Expo '86, the USSR Pavilion exhibit included the **World's largest aircraft**, the Antonov An-124, and the World's largest helicopter, the Mil Mi-26.

Expo '86 had the **world's largest hockey stick** at 60 m (187 ft.) high. The puck with it was 3 m wide x 1 m high (9 ft. x 3 ft.) approximately. In order for a hockey player to use this stick and puck in a normal way, he would have to be 75 m (246 ft.) tall.

The World's **largest gold coin**, worth over one million dollars, was minted to commemorate Expo '86 and was displayed adjacent to the Plaza of Nations.

Expo '86 had the **greatest collection of steam locomotives** since the Chicago Rail Fair in the 1940s.

Vancouver millionaire Jim Pattison got into the Guinness Book of World Records by paying $2,299,000 (US) for John Lennon's psychedelic Rolls-Royce, making it the **most expensive car** in the world. He then donated it to the Province and people of British Columbia at Expo 1986.

There were **642 benches**, each seating 14 people, scattered throughout the Expo '86 site.

There were **4071 seats** in the Expo Theatre.

There were **450 pay telephones** throughout the Expo '86 site.

Canada Post stamp machines at the three main Expo gates sold **$12,000 worth of stamps in** the first five weeks of the fair.

The Scream Machine at Expo carried a total of 1,897,500 riders — an average of 11,500 per day.

Six couples were married at Expo '86 by Shinto Priests.

There were **6,000 ashtrays stolen** from the Ole Cantina Restaurant at Expo (or perhaps they were just taken as souvenirs).

Over 8 million people passed through Lower Mainland border points during Expo, an increase of over 3 million during the same period of 1985.

Expo '86 closed after a **highly successful run of 165 days**. Although the fair started on a wet note and a near normal rainfall of 253 mm occurred during the run, the final day's weather was beautiful. Overall, only 35 days had rain and most fell at night. There was a 53-day dry spell in mid-summer and the last 13 days of the Exposition were rainless.

FOOD

The following list is the total amount of food and drink items sold on the Expo site during the fair. It is not a complete list but is most of the major items.
- 4.2 million hot dogs
- 7.5 million hamburgers
- 1.2 million gallons of beer
- 8 million ice cream products
- 250,000 pounds of coffee
- 3,500 tons of potatoes
- 7 million servings of popcorn
- 35 million litres of soft drinks
- 1 peanut butter and jam sandwich per day (for Jimmy Pattison)

CHAPTER 16

MISCELLANEOUS

GEOGRAPHY

The **geographical centre** of British Columbia is marked by a privately built cairn at Weneez, B.C., a short distance east of Vanderhoof. The name Weneez is a Carrier word meaning "centre."

The **most often used word** in British Columbia geographical place names is "North" (as in North Vancouver, North Fork Granite Creek, etc.) which is used at least 180 times. Not far behind is "Little" (as in Little Fort, Little Mountain, etc.) used about 150 times. Other often used words, and the approximate number of times used, are South (140), Black (125), Beaver (98), Big (80), Green (73), Bear (70) and Copper (40).

The **longest (single word) geographical place name** in British Columbia is Tscheetseneeltaine Creek (also known as Tsini Tsini Creek). It is located in the Coast Mountains and flows north into the Bella Coola River.

There are a great many **"strange and odd" place names** in British Columbia and here are two of the strangest: Qlawd Hill and Qlawdzeet Anchorage. Both names start with a "Q" which is not followed by a "U."

PLACES

A national survey by the University of Lethbridge in 1986, which asked people where or in what province they would prefer to live, showed that, if they could make the move, B.C.'s **population would increase** by about 2.5 million people.

The **first skyscraper** in Vancouver, the Dominion Building, was completed on the northwest corner of Hastings and Cambie in 1909. It is thirteen stories high.

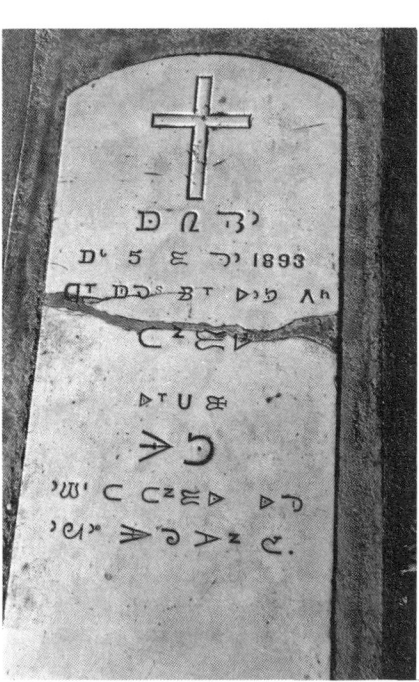

This is one of eight stones in a flower garden in Prince George. Can anyone tell me what the writing says?

The tallest building in B.C. is the Harbour Centre building in Vancouver. It is 177 m (581 ft.) tall, including 30.5 m (100 ft.) pylons, and 32 storeys. The Sheraton-Landmark Hotel in Vancouver is 41 storeys at 120 m (394 ft.). The Royal Bank Tower, also in Vancouver, is 37 storeys at 142.6 m (468ft.).

Vancouver had a **lamplighter** in 1887.

The **first neon signs** in Vancouver were on Granville Street in 1925.

During the 1950s Vancouver had the world's **second greatest amount of neon sign footage**. (Shanghai had the greatest amount.)

The **first pre-sliced bread** was sold in Vancouver at 8 cents a loaf on July 19, 1937.

Located in the southern Chilcotin area of B.C.'s Coast Range Mountains is the Tyak Mountain Lake Resort. It is B.C.'s **newest wilderness resort** and is either a summer or winter paradise depending on your field of activity (hiking, skiing, etc.). It includes a 11,000 m² lodge, which is the largest log structure in B.C.

This monument declares itself to be the Exact Geographical Centre of British Columbia. It is located east of Vanderhoof

PEOPLE

Almost a **third of the immigrants** and refugees coming into Canada every year will eventually settle in B.C.

The **first Japanese immigrant** to Canada was Manzo Nagano. Born in Nagasaki, he stowed away on a ship which landed at New Westminster, May 14, 1877. He eventually settled in Victoria. It has been only since 1868 that emigration from Japan was permitted — prior to that, death was decreed for any Japanese who tried to go abroad.

Forty-six percent of all B.C. homes have fireplaces - the highest figure in Canada. P.E.I. is lowest at eleven %.

Forty-three percent of Canadian households have pets. The population of household pets is highest in Nova Scotia (53%) and lowest in Quebec (36%). The most popular pet is a dog in every province except B.C., where **cats are the favourite**.

Twenty-nine percent of British Columbians do **volunteer work** according to a 1991 survey. The highest in Canada is Alberta at 40% and the lowest is Quebec at 19%. The estimated value of volunteer work in Canada is over $12 billion annually.

The **first nudist society** in Canada was formed in Vancouver in 1938. The "Van Tan Club" established their campground on Grouse Mountain in North Vancouver.

WILDLIFE

There are at least **295 species of birds** that breed in British Columbia, and, including migrants, a total of 448 bird species are known to occur in the province.

There are 16 **species of owls** in Canada and at least 9 of these may be seen in the south Okanagan.

The **second largest concentration of bald eagles** in North America is in the Squamish area of B.C. between Vancouver and Whistler.

The world's **largest black bears** are found on the Queen Charlotte Islands.

Vancouver Island is home to **several thousand black bears**, 700 cougars, more than 2,500 elk and over 100,000 deer.

During early February of 1991 a 400 kg (880 lb.) **bull moose** wandered into the City of Penticton. It became a nuisance and was chased out of town. Three weeks later it came back. Wildlife officials shot it with tranquillizer darts, put it on a sling and called a helicopter. It was taken a considerable distance back into the hills and safely released.

RECORDS

Pat Morrow of Kimberley, B.C., has **climbed the highest mountains on six continents**. Plans for climbing the highest mountain on the only continent he had missed were underway in 1985. (This was for Vinson Massif on Antarctica - 16,860 ft.) I don't know if this climb was accomplished or not. I wrote to him in November 1991 for additional information but my letter was returned from Kimberley unopened, marked address incomplete.

Six elephants escaped from a circus at Cranbrook on the morning of August 6, 1926. Three were recaptured rather quickly and another located, leaving two still missing. It was not until September that one was located at Moyie, but she died before medical aid could help her. The other one, named Charlie Ed, was found and safely recaptured. For his efforts and his month-long journey into the wilds of B.C., the Mayor of Cranbrook rechristened him "Cranbrook Ed."

KERMODEI BEAR

The Kermodei (Kerr-mow-dee) bear of the Terrace area is an attraction of no little proportion to this region. It is white in color, extremely rare and elusive, and also happens to be the Terrace city logo. *Ursus americanus kermodei* is in fact a black bear, and has all the characteristics of a black bear, except for its color. Please remember it is a bear and as such can be extremely dangerous when annoyed or surprised.

Pat Morrow along with a tour group which included Sir Edmund Hillary, the first man to climb Mt. Everest, and Neil Armstrong, the first man to walk on the moon, landed on the **geographical North Pole** in April of 1985. The group consisted of twelve amateur explorers who each paid between $5,000 and $10,000 to join the tour.

Mark Sutton of Victoria set a **new pole sitting record** when he stayed aloft for 488 days, and then sprained his ankle when coming back down. He accomplished this feat for the Paraplegic Association.

Mark Hebbard of Vancouver is the **loudest snorer** in the world and in 1990 was included in the Guinness Book of World Records. His snoring was 10 decibels louder than the level allowed under Vancouver's noise bylaw. His snoring was rated at 90 decibels by testers at the University of British Columbia. He has since had an operation which has toned him down quite a bit.

Powel Janulus of Vancouver, is the **world's greatest polyglot**, having mastered the art of speaking, reading and writing 42 languages.

The world's **pickled-onion eating record** is held by B.C. resident Pat Donohue. In 1978 he consumed 91 pickled onions in one minute, eight seconds.

Bruce McConachy, of West Vancouver, piled up 295 quarters to set the **world coin balancing record**.

The **largest omelet in the world** was cooked up by the Kinsmen's Mother's March in the Hotel Meridien, Vancouver, B.C., on Jan. 27, 1986. The omelet contained 45,000 eggs (3,750 dozen), and was cooked in a pan measuring 13 m x 3 m (43 ft. x 10 ft.). It was entered in the Guinness Book of World Records.

A sick boy from Salt Spring Island, B.C., has set a new world's record for the **number of Christmas cards ever received** by an individual. The eight year old received 205,120 cards for Christmas in 1989.

The **world's biggest sleep-over** was in B.C. Place Stadium when 4,000 Beavers (boys aged five to seven years) spent the night under the dome with their parents (mostly fathers) in April, 1989.

North America's **only stainless steel bobslide** is located 8.5 km (5 mi.) north of Vernon on Highway 97N.

The **only operational and authentic Dutch windmill** in Canada is at Osoyoos, B.C. It was built in 1973. It is inhabited by its owners and is open for tours. It is a replica of one built in Holland around 1816. Windmills were used for grinding grain into flour with stones moved by the force of the wind.

The Cablehouse Restaurant located at Sayward, B.C. "is a **unique steel-frame building** made entirely of used logging cable. The walls contain 8200 ft. of wire rope and weigh almost 26 tons." It was built by Glen Duncan and opened in 1970.

The **longest foot suspension bridge** in the world is the Capilano Suspension Bridge. It is 1.5 m (5 ft.) wide, 137.2 m (450 ft.) long, 70.1 m (230 ft.) high and carries 500,000 people per year. It is located in North Vancouver.

The **second steepest gondola ride** in the world is on Mt. Hays on the outskirts of Prince Rupert.

THE GREAT B.C. CENTENNIAL GOLD COIN TREASURE HUNT

Jars of gold coins and semi-precious coins were buried in the hills west of Avola, as a B.C. Centennial project in 1971. So far they have not been discovered. There are clues and maps available at a nominal charge, from the Kamloops Visitors and Tourist Bureau.

(Update: After the treasure hunt had continued for several years, the Kamloops Daily News became suspicious and tried to find out the truth of the matter. The newspaper even went to the extent of taking the question to court, in order to prove legally that the treasure does exist. That was over three years ago and, to date, "The court case was never concluded, the treasure never found.")

CLOCKS

The **largest cuckoo clock** in North America is located in the town plaza at Kimberley, B.C., the "Bavarian City of the Rockies."

The **only floral clock** in Western Canada is in Polson Park, Vernon, B.C.

On September 24, 1977, the **only steam powered clock** in the world was started up. It is located at Cambie and Water streets in Vancouver and was built by Ray Saunders.

The **tallest clock tower** in B.C. was set in place by a crane at the New Westminster Quay market place on April 21, 1986. It is 22 m (72 ft.) high.

Curtis Scott, of Burnaby, B.C., won an award for a **grandfather clock** he had made out of 30,000 toothpicks.

This is Tintagel Monument located near Burns Lake and named after Tintagel, Cornwall, England. The plaque explains" The central stone in this cairn once formed part of the Norman Walls of Tintagel Castle, reputed birthplace of King Arthur, Knight of the Round Table."

CHAPTER 17

THE ODD SPOT

Approximately five kilometres or so (about three miles) from the Balfour ferry, in the direction of Ainsworth and Kaslo, you will begin to notice **neckties on the telephone and power poles**. These ties, one to a pole, go for almost five kilometres. Apparently this was started about 1980 by a fellow who didn't like the looks of bare poles and decided to brighten them up a bit. I don't know how many he started with, but it seems the cause was taken up by other people and more were soon added. On my last trip down the road I counted 107 ties; five poles in the line were missing their ties. If you are going by that way, count them - see what you get!

The fire hydrants in Kimberly are rather unique. (I'm not sure what the dogs think of them!)

The United Church in Okanagan Falls was originally built in the town of Fairview (near Oliver). It was so strongly and solidly built that in order to move it, in 1929, to its present location, dynamite was "exploded inside the building, to loosen the nails and allow them to transport it in sections, down to the Falls."

◆

In 1909 a **one-eyed man** settled on a rock ridge just south of Bridesville. Then two more one-eyed men settled there and the ridge became known as "One-eyed Mountain." One of them had the reputation of never taking off his overalls. When he bought a new pair he simply pulled them on over the others. They say that at one time he was wearing seven pairs, or the remnants of them, simultaneously.

◆

A **sign on the B.C.–Alaska border** between Hyder, Alaska and Stewart, B.C. states: "All persons (including residents of Canada) entering Canada with goods on which duty and taxes are payable MUST contact Cadada Customs in Prince Rupert." I wonder how many people declare their goods, as Prince Rupert is 465 km (289 m.) away by road?

◆

You seldom see "**Dead End**" **signs** anymore — they mostly have been replaced by "No Exit" and "No Thru Road" signs. The way I heard it was like this: A "Dead End" sign was put up on a street that had a dead end: a cemetary. Some people failed to see the humour of the situation and complained about it.

◆

Some of the **more interesting signs** found in B.C. are: "PET PIT STOP" found by an empty field near Liard Hot Springs; " NO SWIMMING OR DIVING OF ANY KIND" placed right below a sign which states "SEWAGE OUTFALL LOCATED APPROX. 300 FEET BELOW WATER LINE" at the Earl Cove Ferry Terminal; and "HIGHWAY SERVES AS EMERGENCY AIRSTRIP NEXT 2 KM", wich is found on the Cassiar Highway.

SODA SPRINGS

At a point 4.8 km (2.9 mi.) west of Kaslo, on Highway 31A, there is a natural soda spring. Soda water bubbles up out of the ground at this point. The water is crystal clear, cool, and very good to drink, if you like soda water. The stain on the ground here is from chemical changes which take place when the water is released from its underground pressures and exposed to air. The same changes occur if you bottle the water. It turns cloudy and a sediment settles on the bottom of the bottle. It is still good to drink but tastes better if refrigerated.

CHAPTER 18

ODDS & ENDS

THE METRIC SYSTEM

In Canada, measurements are made using the **metric system**. Rain, snowfall, windspeed and visibility are all expressed in metric units. Temperature is calculated on the Celsius scale. All distance markers and road speed signs are in kilometres (km) and kilometres per hour (km/h).

◆

Gasoline and other **liquid volumes** or commodities are measured in litres. For normal everyday use, there are three basic units of measurement in the metric system: the metre, the gram and the litre.

- *The metre (m) is used for measuring lengths and distances.*
- *The gram (g) is used for measuring weights and mass.*
- *The litre (L) is used for measuring capacity.*
- *A 10-centimetre cube will hold 1 litre of water and it will weigh 1 kilogram.*

There are six numerical prefixes which can be used in conjunction with the three basic units named above. These are:

- *milli, meaning one-thousandth (1/1,000 or 0.001)*
- *centi, meaning one-hundredth (1/100 or 0.01)*
- *deci, meaning one-tenth (1/10 or 0.1)*
- *deka, meaning ten (10)*
- *hecto, meaning one hundred (100)*
- *kilo, meaning one thousand (1,000)*

For normal, average, everyday use, only three prefixes will likely be needed: milli, centi and kilo. For measuring **lengths and distances** all three are in common use: millimetre (mm), centimetre (cm) and kilometre (km). The metre consists of 1,000 mm or 100 cm - it's just a matter of moving the decimal point.

The push buttons on a telephone are 1 cm square (1 cm²).
The TV Guide measures approximately 13 cm by 19 cm.
The standard egg carton is about 30 cm long.
The front page of the Vancouver Province is about 30 cm by 35 cm.
The front page of the Vancouver Sun is about 35 cm by 60 cm.
A 26-inch TV screen is about 52 cm by 40 cm.
The average doorway is about 2 metres high.

For longer distances the kilometre is used. This is one thousand metres and is equal to eight or ten average city blocks.

For measuring weight we normally only use the basic units of grams (g), and kilograms (kg).

An average loaf of bread is about 450 g.
The TV Guide weighs about 100 g.
A desk telephone is about 2 kg.

An average man is 165 to 180 cm in height and weighs 70 to 80 kg.
You may use milligrams (mg) when dealing with medicines. An average aspirin tablet weighs about 325 mg.

For **measuring capacities** we use mainly the litre (L) and/or millilitre (mL).

A teaspoon holds 5 mL.
A cup contains 250 mL.
An average can of pop contains 355 mL.
A bottle of beer contains 341 mL.
The gas tank of the average car holds 50 to 60 L.
A barrel contains 205 L.

There is one more type of measurement that concerns us in everyday use: **temperature**. This is measured in degrees Celsius (°C). In this system, 0°C is the freezing point of water and 100°C is the boiling point.

A nice spring day would be 15°C.
A hot day would be 30°C and over.
Normal body temperature is 37°C.
A slow oven would be around 130°C.
A very hot oven would be around 275°C.
There is one point on the scales where the Fahrenheit and Celsius temperatures are the same: -40°.

You notice I have left out the scales for converting from one system to the other. The reason for this is simple: the best way to learn metric is to think metric. Use the above examples for comparison purposes and discover that it is not that complicated.

TIME CHANGES IN BRITISH COLUMBIA

All clocks should be set one hour ahead at 1:00 am on the first Sunday in April and one hour back at 1:00 am on the last Sunday in October. "Spring forward, fall back."

MESSAGES AND CONGRATULATIONS

Are you or is someone you know celebrating one of the following events? Messages and congratulations will be received from:

Her Majesty, the Queen, for anniversaries of 60 years or more, and birthdays of 100 years or more.

The Governor General, for anniversaries from 50 to 59 years, and birthdays from 90 to 99 years.

The Prime Minister, for anniversaries of 50 years or more, and birthdays of 70 years or more.

The Lieutenant Governor, for anniversaries of 50 years or more, and birthdays of 70 years or more.

The Premier of the Province, for anniversaries of 50 years or more, and birthdays of 70 years or more.

Requests for these must be made well in advance. For more information contact your local MP or MLA or write (postage free) to the House of Commons, Ottawa, Ontario or to the Provincial Secretary's Office, Parliament Buildings, Victoria, B.C.

ANNIVERSARIES

	Traditional	**Modern**
First	Paper	Clocks
Second	Cotton	China
Third	Leather	Crystal, Glass
Fourth	Fruit, Flowers	Appliances
Fifth	Wood	Silverware
Sixth	Candy, Iron	Wood
Seventh	Wool, Copper	Desk Sets
Eighth	Bronze, Pottery	Linens, Laces
Ninth	Pottery, Willow	Leather
Tenth	Tin, Aluminum	Diamond Jewelry
Eleventh	Steel	Fashion Jewelry
Twelfth	Silk, Linen	Pearls
Thirteenth	Lace	Textiles, Furs
Fourteenth	Ivory	Gold Jewelry
Fifteenth	Crystal	Watches
Twentieth	China	Platinum
Twenty-fifth	Silver	Silver
Thirtieth	Pearl	Diamond
Thirty-fifth	Coral	Jade
Fortieth	Ruby	Ruby
Forty-fifth	Sapphire	Sapphire
Fiftieth	Gold	Gold
Fifty-fifth	Emerald	Emerald
Sixtieth	Diamond	Diamond
Seventy-fifth	Diamond	Diamond

STATUTORY HOLIDAYS IN B.C.

New Years Day
  January 1
Good Friday
  Friday preceding Easter
Easter Monday
  Monday after Easter Sunday
Victoria Day
  Monday preceding May 24
Canada Day
  July 1
B.C. Day
  First Monday in August
Labour Day
  First Monday in September
Thanksgiving Day
  Second Monday in October
Remembrance Day
  November 11
Christmas Day
  December 25
Boxing Day
  December 26

BIRTHSTONES AND FLOWERS

	Birthstone	Flower
January	Garnet	Carnation
February	Amethyst	Violet
March	Aquamarine	Jonquil
April	Diamond	Sweet Pea
May	Emerald	Lily of the Valley
June	Pearl	Rose
July	Ruby	Larkspur
August	Peridot	Gladiolus
September	Sapphire	Aster
October	Opal	Calendula
November	Topaz	Chrysanthemum
December	Turquoise	Narcissus

ANSWERS TO PLACE NAMES QUIZ ON PAGE 70

1. Cawston
2. Greenwood
3. Blubber Bay
4. Williams Lake
5. Trail
6. Balfour
7. Stewart
8. Victoria
9. Ocean Falls
10. Yale
11. Soda Creek
12. Pavilion
13. Mission
14. Likely
15. Rutland
16. Armstrong
17. Wonowon
18. Penticton
19. Sunset Prairie
20. Crowsnest
21. Hope
22. Kitimat
23. Bridesville
24. Merritt
25. Shoreacres
26. Grand Forks
27. Cascade
28. Wells
29. Sicamous
30. Skookumchuck
31. Progress
32. Salmon Arm
33. Abbotsford
34. Boston Bar
35. Needles
36. Shuswap
37. Adams Lake
38. Kingsgate
39. Gold Bridge
40. Chilliwack
41. Rogers Pass
42. Taylor
43. Port Mellon
44. Terrace
45. Miracle Beach
46. Slocan
47. Alert Bay
48. Princeton
49. Revelstoke
50. Midway
51. Approximately 150 islands and islets.
52. A few centimetres (not much more than a ripple in the creek).
53. Sir Alexander Mackenzie.
54. On Highway No. 2 (northeastern B.C.).
55. Barkerville and Fort Steele.
56. It is the first two letters of the areas three main industries: Fishing, Logging and Mining.
56. The Columbia and Yukon Rivers.

A man from Toronto had led a good life;
He was ninety years old when he died.
He went straight to heaven and when he got their
He was shown all around by a guide.

The Guide was no less than St Peter himself
And the sights were all great to behold,
Until they spied a large column of folk
All in chains and their story was told.

"You see," said St. Peter, "these folks must be chained
Tho' we've told them there's nothing they'll lack;
They're all from B.C. and tho' Heaven is fine
They persistently try to go back!"

Arlee Anderson
Castlegar, B.C.

BIBLIOGRAPHY

The following sources were referred to in compiling the information contained in this book:

According to Guinness
A Conspectus of Canada - 1967
Alberta Bingo News
Alberta Native News
Alberta Report
Alexander Mackenzie Heritage Trail (brochure)
Atlas of B.C.
Atlin (brochure)
Atlin Claim (newspaper)

B.C. A History
B.C. Bookworld
B.C. Business Magazine
B.C. Calling
B.C. Centennial Record
B.C. Chronicle
B.C. Facts
B.C. Historical Quarterly
B.C. Hydro Service Digest
B.C. Industrial Review
B.C. Its History, People, Commerce
B.C. Outdoors Magazine
B.C. Pioneer Years
B.C. Ports Handbook
B.C. Road Map
B.C. Rockies
B.C. Telephone Facts 1991
B.C. Tourist Accommodation Guide
B.C. Traveller's Handbook
BCTV News
Barbizon Magazine
Barkerville
Beyond Garibaldi
Blakeburn - From Dust to Dust, Blake
Burnaby Community Directory
Burnaby Now Newspaper

Bygones of Burnaby
CBC -TV
CHEK Channel 6 TV
CJJC Radio
CKWX Radio
CNR Magazine "Keeping Track"
CTV News
Camper News, West Kootenay, Boundary, Revelstoke
Campfire Sketches of the Cariboo
Canada Quiz and Game Book, Fisher
Canada's V.C.'s
Canada West Magazine
Canadian Almanac
Canadian Handbook
Canadian Link Newspaper
Canadian Weather Calendar
Capsule Story of Lillooet
Castlegar News
City of New Westminster
Columbia Valley Visitors Guide
Community Profile Magazine
Coquitlam, Poco, Port Moody, Pitt Meadows, Maple Ridge News

Data Bank Canada Map 1989
Daytrippers Paradise - Hope and Fraser Canyon Guide
Discover an Aluminum Legend (brochure)
Discover Barkerville
Discover Kootenay County
Discover the Queen Charlotte Islands
Driving the Alaska Highway, 1990

Eastender News
Edmonton Examiner Newspaper

Edmonton Journal
Edmonton Sun
Equinox Magazine
Expo 86 (promotional material)

Facts 1990
Flying High (Van. Int. Airport 50 yr. book)
Forestry Forum
Fort St. James (brochure)
Four Seasons Vacation Land Road Map
Four Walls In The West, Scott
Frontier Guides
Fur and Gold

Gazetteer of Canada (B.C.) 1953 & 1966
Ghost Camps
Ghost Towns and Drowned Towns of West Kootenay
Golden Moments of Hope
Gold In The Cariboo
Gold Rush Trail
Greater Vancouver Regional District (GVRD) News
Guide to Gold Panning in B.C.
Guinness Book of World Records

Help yourself survive an earthquake
Henderson's B.C. Directory
Heritage Cemeteries in B.C.
Heritage Log, The West (Nat. Parks)
Highway Information Signs
History of B.C.
History of Hockey in B.C.
History of New Westminster

Holidayer - Okanagan Guide

Introducing Sayward (brochure)
It's All Ours - Canada

Kamloops Daily News
Kamloops Sentinel, The
Kootenay Country, The Great Escape
Kootenay Lake Adventure Guide

Milepost, The
Milestones of Vancouver Island
Mission Visitors Guide
Moyie Reflections
Municipal Road Signs

National and Historic Parks Guide - B.C. and Alta.
Neighbors Newspapers
New Westminster Now Newspaper

Okanagan Lake Westside
Okanagan-Similkameen Guide
Okanagan Travel Guide
Old Farmers Almanac
1001 B.C. Place Names

Parks Companion (National Parks Guide)
Performance Magazine (Canada Post)
Prince Rupert City Map and Guide
Principal Trees of B.C.

Provincial Report (B.C. Gov't News)
Provincial Road Signs

Quick Canadian Facts
Quick Facts About B.C.

Reader's Digest
Revelstoke Dam (brochure)
Royal Bank Reporter
Royal City Record

Sagas West Magazine
Science Digest
Shipwrecks of B.C.
South Moresby News
Stewart/Hyder (brochure)
Summer Scene - Shuswap Country

Tatogga Lake Resort (brochure)
The British Columbian
The Butchart Gardens (brochure)
The Canadian World Almanac
The Columbian Newspaper
The Courts of British Columbia (brochure)
The Daily Columbian Newspaper
The land of long summers
The Last Spike
The Okanagan, Peachy
The Province Newspaper
The Province TV Times
The Story of Okanagan Falls

The Storyteller, Alberta Provincial Museum
The Sun Newspaper
The Sunny Okanagan
The Surrey Story
The Valley of the Ghosts
The Westender News
The World Almanac and Book of Facts
This Is Beautiful British Columbia
Thompson Country
Three Valley Gap (brochure)
Top of the Okanagan - Things to do
Tweedsmuir Provincial Park (brochure)

Valley of the Ghosts
Victoria and Vancouver Island Visitors Guide
Victoria Chamber of Commerce
Visitor's Guide to Prince George

Westerly Guide - Pacific Rim National Park
Westworld Magazine
Woodlands Family Newsletter
Would You Believe 9,000 years

You and your Environment
Yukon Highway Map
Yukon News Visitors Guide 1991

Also see the list of people and places which provided information for the book, under the acknowledgements.

ABOUT THE AUTHOR

Don Blake was born and raised in British Columbia. Before becoming a writer he worked in construction, in the trucking industry, as a longshoreman and as a prospector. He also served with the RCAF. His previous books are: *Blakeburn: From Dust to Dust*, a history of a coal mining town; *This is Beautiful British Columbia*, a book of B.C. trivia, which has been updated, revised and reprinted here as *B.C. Trivia*; *The Valley of the Ghosts* which has been slightly revised and reprinted as *Valley of the Ghosts*, a history of the "Silvery" Slocan area of the West Kootenays; and *Alberta Trivia*.

INDEX

A
Abbotsford 24, 39, 67
Adams River 47
Aggassiz 72
Ainsworth 85
Albion 28
Alert Bay 42
Amor De Cosmos 19
Amor de Cosmos 18
Anderson Lakes 29
Annacis Island 35
Armstrong 20, 77
Ashcroft 53
Atlin 44, 67
Atlin Lake 31

B
Babine Lake 47
Balfour 29
Ballou, Billy 32
Bannister, Roger 58
Barker, Doug 67
Barkerville 23, 33, 49, 57, 67
Barkley, Charles William 15
Barkley, Frances 15
Barry, James 60
Barry, R. 29
Begbie, Matthew 17, 22, 60
Begg, Frank 33
Begg, Fred 33
Belcher, A.T. 62
Bell, Gordon and Ethel 69
Bell, Marilyn 58
Bella Coola 15
Bendickson, Dennis 42
Bennett, Bill 50
Bishop Demers 26
Blanchet, Father F.N. 23
Blanshard, Richard 18
Blessing, Charles 60
Bligh, Wiliam 15
Boeing, William 37
Boston Bar 35
Boyd, Rob 56
Bralorne 43
Bridesville 85

Britannia Beach 35, 53
Brothers, F.P. 30
Bryant, John 38
Buchan, John,
    1st Baron of Tweedsmuir 75
Burnaby 24, 25, 49, 62, 84
Burns Lake 63
Burrard Inlet 25, 28, 32

C
Cameron, "Cariboo" 33
Campbell River 40
Cantryn, Marjorie 62
Cape Flattery 28
Cape St. James 52
Cariboo 19, 59, 60
Carnation Creek 54
Carroll, R.W. 19
Cassiar 44, 54, 85
Cassidy, Ellen 49
Castlegar 21, 64
Centreville 44, 67
Chemainus 67
Chilcotin 81
Chilliwack 72
Chinook Cove 53
Clark, Charles 20
Clayburn 67
Clinton 60
Cloverdale 62
Coalmont 34
Cody, Henry 75
Columbia Lake 64
Comox 49
Cook, James 15
Coquihalla Highway 34
Coquitlam 35
Cornwall, C.F. 19
Cortes, John 58
Coward, Elizabeth "Betty" 61
Coward, Jim 61
Craigellachie 30, 31
Cranbrook 32, 33, 46, 53, 82
Creston 35, 48
Cultus 72
Cumberland 67

D
Dawson City 25
de la Bodega y Quadra,
    Juan Francisco 26
Delasalle, Philip 58
Demers, Father Modeste 23
Dempsey, Lew 62
Di Nava, Father Lopez 22
Diaz, Father Mario 22
Dollarton 78
Donald 23
Donohue, Pat 83
Douglas 14
Douglas, David 41
Douglas, James 17, 18, 20
Drake, Francis 15
Duncan 62, 67
Duncan, Glen 83
Dunn, Jimmy 65
Dutch Creek 46

E
Eason, Gordon 42
East Kootenay 64
Eastman, George 64
Edwards, Ralph 75
Emory Bar 30
Erxleber, Heather 55
Esquimalt 18, 25, 29, 55

F
Fairmont 46
Fairview 85
Fan, Harry 61
Fitzgerald, W.F. 60
Flynn, William 30
Fort Alexandria 16
Fort Langley 16, 17, 28, 45,
    49, 50
Fort Nelson 37, 45, 59, 67
Fort Rupert 43
Fort St. James 47, 56, 67, 74
Fort St. John 37, 45
Fort Steele 78
Fort Victoria 32
Fort Yale 32

Fortune, Alexander Leslie 47
François Lake 51
Fraser Canyon 31, 35
Fraser Lake 31, 44
Fraser River 30, 32, 35, 36, 64
Fraser, Simon 16, 64
Freeman, Alfred 44

G

Gabriola Island 19
Galbraith's Ferry 61
George, Dan 78
Georgia Strait 17
Gibson, W.W. 36
Glacier National Park 54
Godfrey, A. Earl 37
Gold Harbour 16
Golden 23, 46
Golden Ears Provincial Park 40
Graham Island 63
Grand Forks 57, 65
Gray Creek 66
Greene, Nancy 56
Greenwood 66

H

Hallberg, Mrs. Lee 66
Hamilton, Charles 36
Hare, Alex 60
Harmon, Daniel William 47
Harrison 72
Harrison, Rusty 65
Harvie, Claude 34
Haynes, John 48
Hazleton 78
Hebbard, Mark 83
Hell's Gate 27
Helmcken, Dr. J.S. 22
Henderson Lake 53
Hepburn, Douglas 58
Hill, Samuel 14
Hope 32, 33, 34, 45, 72
Horseshoe Bay 35
Houghton, Chas. F. 19
Houston 44

I - J

Invermere 16
Island View 15
Janulus, Powel 83
Jericho 59
Jericho Beach 37, 38
Jessop, John 20
Joe, Andrew 61
Johnson, Ed 58
Johnson, Rita 19
Juan de Fuca Strait 12, 16, 28
Jung, Douglas 19

K

Kamloops 16, 19, 35, 53, 56, 60, 61
Kaslo 27, 71, 85
Kelowna 38, 48, 65, 67, 76
Kermode, Francis 68
Kicking Horse Pass 30
Kimberley 44, 67, 82, 84
Kimpton, Rufus 23
Kitchener 35
Kitimat 44, 76
Kootenay Bay 29

L

Lake Windemere 24
Lakelse 54
Langley 39
Leanard McLure, Leanard 18
Lee, Kwong 49
Liard 85
Lillooet 47, 49, 53, 67
Little Fort 81
Little Mountain 81
Little Tokyo 21
Long Beach 66, 73
Lowe, W.H. 48
Lowry, Malcolm 78
Lynn Valley 42
Lytton 30, 46, 53, 60

M

MacDonald, W.J. 19
MacKay, John 15
MacKenzie, Alexander 15
MacLeod, Earl L. 38
Magnussen, Karen 58
Maguinna 16
Maple Ridge 49, 66
Marble, Charles 36
Marchand, Len 19
Martin, Mrs. Emily 49
Martinez, Jose 22
Masset 68
Matheson, Roger 37
McBride, Richard 18, 55
McConachie, Grant 37
McConachy, Bruce 83
McCreight, John Foster 18
McDermott, Mrs. William 49
McGill, Helen Emma (Gregory) 61
McInnes Island 53
McKey, Alys 37
McKinley, William 33
McLean, Allan 60
McLean, Archie 60
McLean, Charles 60
McLean, Hector 60
McMillan, James 16

McMurphy, Sgt. James 32
Meares, John 16
Merritt 34, 66
Miller, Jonathan 60
Millstream 40, 49
Miner, Bill 61
Mission 24, 61, 78
Mitchell, Walter 38
Mitchell's Harbour 16
Moberly, Walter 69
Monte Creek 61
Moodyville 50
Moore, Linda 58
Moresby Island 63
Moricetown 46, 68
Morrow, Pat 82
Moses, Wellington Delaney 49
Mount Meager 46
Mt. Fairweather 12
Mt. Logan 12
Mt. Robson 12
Mt. Waddington 12

N

Nagano, Manzo 82
Nanaimo 22, 29, 30, 34, 65, 77
Nathan, Henry 19
Nelson 25, 27, 50, 57, 68
Nelson, Hugh 19
New Denver 71
New Hazelton. 68
New Westminster 17, 18, 19, 22, 25, 27, 28, 30, 31, 32, 36, 44, 49, 61, 68, 77, 79, 82, 84
Nicola Valley 66
Nootka Sound 16
North Bend 35
North Delta 35
North Vancouver 32, 83

O

Okanagan 48, 50, 52, 53, 54, 82
Okanagan Falls 72, 85
Okanagan Landing 27
Okanagan Valley 16, 46, 48
O'Leary, William 27
Oling, Garry 66
O'Neil, Garry 56
Osoyoos 48, 52, 65, 83
Owen, Walter S. 18

P

Palmer, Francis 61
Parker, Marion 42
Paton, Helen 61
Pattullo, Thomas Duff 57
Pattullo, Thomas H. 57
Pemberton 53

Penticton 54, 57, 77, 78, 82
Peterson, Bertha 61
Phillips, Dave 56
Pointer Island 29
Pope John Paul II 24
Port Alberni 40
Port Clements 41
Port Edward 47, 74
Port McNeill 42
Port Moody 30, 45
Port Renfrew 18
Powell, I.W. 18
Premier John Oliver 14
Prince George 21, 31, 37, 38, 39, 41, 68
Prince George. 76
Prince Rupert 28, 35, 42, 47, 68, 83, 85
Princeton 32, 34, 45

Q

Qlawd Hill 81
Qlawdzeet Anchorage 81
Queen Charlotte Islands 12, 17, 35, 37, 41, 44, 45, 52, 62, 63, 73, 82
Queen Elizabeth 35
Queen Victoria 17
Quesne 33
Quesnel 49

R

Race Rocks 29
Red Creek 53
Rev. E. Cridge 22
Rev. Henry "Father Pat" Irwin 24
Revelstoke 23, 51, 54, 56, 69
Revis, Joseph 49
Rhodes, Brian 58
Richfield 49, 60
Richmond 36, 49, 50, 58
Riondel 43
Rithet Creek 42
Rogers, Albert 29
Rogers Pass 30, 35, 54
Rolston, Tilly 19
Romilly, Selwyn 61
Ronald, Barbara 15
Ross, Alexander 16
Rossland 44, 50, 56, 68
Rykert, John C. 48

S

Saanich 15
Salmo 25, 35
Salt Spring Island 83
San Juan Islands 17

Sapperton 22
Sardis 38
Saunders, Charles 36
Saunders, Ray 84
Sayward 78, 83
Schmidt, Dolores 39
Scott, Curtis 84
Searles, Ed 61
Seton 29
Seymour Falls 53
Seymour, Frederick 17, 18
Shawnigan Lake 58
Shoemaker, Willie 58
Shore, David 37
Shorts, T.D. 27
Sihota, Moe 18
Silverdale 61
Slocan 43
Smith, Bill 18
Smith, Donald A. 30, 31
Smith, Mary Ellen 19
Smith River 54
Smithers 59, 68, 79
Soda Creek 60
Sooke Lake 42
South Moresby 73
Sparwood 44
Squamish 35, 53
St. Germain, Doris Elva 62
Stanley Park 27, 40
Stark. Olive 37
Steele, Colonel Samuel 61
Stewart 43, 53, 68, 72, 85
Stuart, David 16
Sullivan, John H. 60
Sumas Canal 53
Sunshine Coast 42
Surrey 31, 34, 35, 41, 42, 48, 62, 68, 76
Sutton, Julie 58
Sutton, Mark 83
Swanson Bay 53

T

Taku 31
Tanemura, Roy 38
Tanner, Elaine 58
Tate, Ned 60
Tchesinkut Lake 63
Terrace 46, 61, 68
Thompson, David 16
Thompson, J.S. 19
Three Valley Gap 68
Tofino 62
Tolmie, S.F. 38
Trail 44, 64
Triangle Island 29

Trim, George 37
Trutch, Joseph W. 19
Tsawwassen 29
Tscheetseneeltaine Creek 81
Tumbler Ridge 31, 69

U

Ucluelet 53, 66
Upper Skeena 42
Ussher, John 60

V

Van Horne, Cornelius 30
Van Horne, Sir William 30, 69
Vancouver 14, 22, 25, 26, 28, 29, 30, 31, 32, 33, 34, 35, 36, 37, 38, 39, 40, 42, 43, 45, 53, 54, 55, 57, 58, 59, 61, 62, 65, 69, 76, 77, 78, 79, 81, 83
Vancouver, George 15, 16, 26
Vancouver Island 12, 13, 15, 17, 18, 19, 26, 28, 42, 45, 63, 73, 82
Vander Zalm, Bill 19
Vanderhoek, Marty 51
Vanderhoof 31, 69, 81
Vernon 25, 46, 55, 69, 83, 84
Victoria 16, 17, 19, 20, 22, 25, 26, 28, 29, 30, 33, 34, 36, 37, 39, 42, 49, 50, 52, 53, 54, 57, 58, 69, 74, 83

W

Walachin 55
Wallace, Robert 19
Weneez 81
West Vancouver 35, 50
Westbank 69
Westley, Daniel 58
Whistler 56
Wichmann, Heinz 66
Wickheim, Jube 58
Williams Creek 22
Williams Lake 69
Williams, Percy 58
Windermere 33
Winfield 50
Wing, Peter 19

Y - Z

Yahk 35
Yale 19, 29, 30, 32, 35, 43, 49, 60
Zilke, Earl 39

Other Books From Lone Pine Publishing

Discover's Guide: Fraser River Delta — Don Watmough

A recreational and nature guide to over forty sites along this ecological and economic lifeblood of southwestern British Columbia, from Boundary Bay to Pitt River. Full colour photos and maps.

$12.95 softcover   128 pp.   5 1/2 x 8 1/2   ISBN 1-55105-014-5

Plants of Northern British Columbia — MacKinnon, Pojar, Coupé

A handy reference guide to common plants of the northern interior region of B.C. for the amateur or professional botanist, naturalist, or forester. Includes keys, conspectuses, and detailed notes on ethnobotanical and etymological information for each species. Full-colour photos and line drawings.

$19.95 softcover   352 pp.   5 1/2 x 8 1/2   ISBN 1-55105-015-3

Bicycling Vancouver — Volker Bodegom

A must for all Vancouver and area cyclists, this touring guidebook includes over 30 routes in and around Vancouver from Horseshoe Bay east to New Westminster and Delta. Each route includes a map and a detailed road log. Information on clothing, equipment, safety, different types of cycling, advocacy, and clubs is included in the extensive reference section. Maps, photographs.

$14.95 softcover   208 pp.   5 1/2 x 8 1/2   ISBN 1-55105-012-9

Gardening in Vancouver — Judy Newton

Tailored to Vancouver's soil and climate conditions, and intended for both intermediate and home gardeners. Contains two full-colour sections with expert hints for successful gardening. Full-colour photographs, illustrations.

$14.95 softcover   176 pp.   5 1/2 x 8 1/2   ISBN 0-919433-74-X

Picnic Guide to British Columbia — Nancy Gibson & John Whittaker

An entertaining and unusual guide to picnicking, including details of local history and providing suggestions on things to see, to do, and (most importantly) to eat. Forty site, maps, and photographs.

$11.95   264 pp.   5 1/2 x 8 1/2   ISBN 0-919433-59-6

Ocean to Alpine: A British Columbia Nature Guide — Joy & Cam Finlay

Explore Wildlife and nature viewing sites from Vancouver Island to the Kootenays in this comprehensive guide. Six area maps, 592 locations and 32 pages of full-colour photographs.

$14.95 softcover   256 pp.   5 1/2 x 8 1/2   ISBN 1-55105-013-X

Buy these and other books from your local bookstore or order directly from Lone Pine Publishing, #206, 10426 - 81 Avenue, Edmonton, Alberta T6E 1X5. Phone: (403) 433-9333 Fax: (403) 433-9646